AMERICA'S FAVORITE DESSERTS

Sara Lee®

Quick, easy-to-make, fun, festive desserts from America's best-known name in desserts.

Copyright © 1992 by Sara Lee Bakery, Chicago, Illinois.
Sara Lee Corporation has the exclusive right to use the trademarks:
SARA LEE
AMERICA'S FAVORITE DESSERTS
NOBODY DOESN'T LIKE SARA LEE
All rights reserved, including the right to reproduce this work, or any portion thereof, in any form whatsoever without written permission from Sara Lee Bakery.

Printed and bound in the United States of America.

Cover photo recipe, Chocolate Raspberry Dobosch Torte, found on page 40.

Special thanks to Sara Lee Bakery for their expertise, creativity, and support: Paul Lustig, President; Dave Bryan, Senior Vice President, Retail; Rich Seban, Director of Marketing; and Colleen Gillespie, Group Brand Manager.

Copy Writing and Art Direction: Wheatley Blair, Inc., Chicago, IL
Food Styling: Wheatley Blair, Inc., Chicago, IL
Recipe Development and Testing: Wheatley Blair, Inc., Chicago, IL
Editor: Jan Carlton, J & B Editions, Publishers, Norfolk, VA
Photography: Sam Griffith Studio, Inc. , Chicago, IL
Cover and Book Design: Scott Wampler, Opal Arts, Chicago, IL
Illustrations: Scott Wampler, Opal Arts, Chicago, IL
Publisher: J & B Editions, Publishers, Norfolk, VA

Photos on pages 9, 11, 15, 17, 19, 79 reprinted by permission from HOUSE BEAUTIFUL, copyright © June, 1992,
The Hearst Corporation. All rights reserved.
David Frazier, photographer.

Recipes selected from Sara Lee Bakery's "America's Best Dessert" recipe contest. Additional recipes developed by Wheatley Blair, Inc., and contributed by Chefs:

Philippe Boulot, The Mark Hotel, New York
Robert Del Grande, Cafe Annie, Houston
Christopher Gross, Christopher's, Phoenix
Mary Beth Liccioni, Le Francais, Chicago
Jean-Louis Palladin, Jean-Louis At The Watergate, Washington, D.C.
Nancy Silverton, Campanile, Los Angeles
Joachim Splichal, Patina, Los Angeles
Jacques Torres, Le Cirque, New York

Deepest thanks and appreciation to all contributing chefs.

FOREWORD

"Nobody Doesn't Like Sara Lee" is widely recognized as one of the most memorable statements created about Sara Lee frozen baked goods. It still rings true because Sara Lee Bakery has stood for quality since our founding in 1949. Sara Lee quality means great taste, so you can have confidence that our baked goods make a terrific base for these exciting new dessert recipes.

Some of America's best-known culinary experts sampled and selected many of the recipes included in this cookbook. We hope you'll discover how easy it is to take our frozen baked goods, and with a little imagination, make delicious desserts appropriate for everyday, special occasions, family meals, holidays, brunch, or after-school snacks.

Enjoy!

Sara Lee

CONTENTS

INTRODUCTION

This book is about simple, creative, easy-to-make desserts that use Sara Lee baked goods as a base. There are recipes for chocolate lovers and fruit fanatics, as well as treats for the children. Additionally, there are sweet temptations for everyday, holidays, and ideas for brunch — a wide variety of sweet sensations you can prepare at home.

With today's lifestyles, finding time to make desserts from scratch can be difficult. AMERICA'S FAVORITE DESSERTS makes dessert preparation quicker and easier to do, so you can enjoy sweets more often and get out of the kitchen faster. Whether for everyday, family and holiday events, or a delightful snack, Sara Lee is ready when you are, bakery fresh in your freezer.

A Taste For All Reasons

Desserts featured in Chapter One include the finalists selected from thousands of recipes created by home cooks who entered Sara Lee Bakery's "America's Best Dessert" recipe contest. In fact, contest recipes appear throughout this book. Chapter Two includes desserts you can serve everyday, any day, to give at-home meals a sweet reward.

When only the best will do, Chapter Three helps you make special occasions even more special. Chapter Four will get your holiday dessert plans underway, while Chapter Five covers snacks you can have on hand whenever the sweet tooth strikes. Chapter Six offers dessert secrets from America's top chefs, and Chapter Seven gives brunch a delicious boost.

Home cooking enthusiasts from across the nation, America's top chefs, and Sara Lee Bakery's food professionals contributed many luscious recipe ideas to AMERICA'S FAVORITE DESSERTS.

Dessert, The Sweet Thing in Life

Everyone has a sweet tooth. We're born with it. Sweets are a reward, they give us pleasure and enjoyment. What was once savored centuries ago only by Kings, Queens, and royalty, Sara Lee has brought to families all across America. Desserts bring smiles because they taste good, and delicious taste has been the focal point of Sara Lee Bakery's heritage.

That heritage is supported by a commitment to using only top quality, pure food ingredients. There are no preservatives in Sara Lee baked goods because they are flash-frozen right out of the oven to lock in flavor and texture.

You can be sure the recipes featured in this book have met Sara Lee's high taste and quality standards, so you can continue to say, "Nobody Doesn't Like Sara Lee."

We hope you enjoy this book and that it brings you many happy dessert experiences. From our family to yours, happy desserting!

If you have comments or questions, please write Sara Lee Bakery, 224 South Michigan, Chicago, Illinois 60604. Or call toll-free 1-800-323-7117.

1 AMERICA'S FAVORITE DESSERTS

Thousands of home cooking enthusiasts entered Sara Lee Bakery's "America's Best Dessert" contest by creating recipes that use Sara Lee Pound Cake as a base. Through public voting to select a winner, the verdict was announced in HOUSE BEAUTIFUL: America's Favorite Dessert is Italian Biscotti Crescent cookies, submitted by Marie Serena of Campbell, California. This was the first national recipe contest to choose the winner by popular vote.

Finalists also included: Caramel Cinnamon Huts by Linda Ervin of Landis, North Carolina; Mocha Mousse Crunch Cake by Kim Happel of Louisville, Kentucky; Amaretto Truffle Torte by Rita Reimer of Idialantic, Florida; and Peach Melba Cloud by Vonnerie Wood of Marshall, Michigan. Congratulations to all.

The above five recipes were selected on the basis of presentation, originality, ease of preparation, and of course, taste by seven of America's top chefs.

Now you can make America's Favorite Desserts and pick your favorite.

ITALIAN BISCOTTI CRESCENTS

about 2 dozen cookies

The winning recipe from Sara Lee's "America's Best Dessert" contest.

Preheat oven to 350°F.

1 (10 3/4-ounce) Sara Lee Pound Cake, thawed
1/2 cup cinnamon graham cracker crumbs (approximately 6 squares, crushed)
1/2 cup unblanched almonds
1/3 cup butter or margarine, melted
1/4 cup finely chopped red and green candied cherries (2 tablespoons *each*)
1 1/2 teaspoons anise extract
Powdered sugar, as needed

Place Pound Cake pieces in a food processor or blender container; cover and process or blend until pieces are coarse crumbs. Add graham cracker crumbs and almonds; cover and process or blend again until the texture of sand. Transfer crumbs to a medium bowl; stir in butter, candied cherries, and anise extract, blending well until mixture holds together.

Shape rounded tablespoons of mixture into crescent shapes on an ungreased 15 x 10 x 1-inch baking pan. Bake for 20 to 25 minutes or until lightly browned. Cool on baking sheets until firm. Cookies harden as they cool. Remove and roll *each* cookie in powdered sugar, coating well.

Variations: Dip one end of baked biscotti into melted white or dark chocolate and sprinkle with finely chopped almonds.

Marie Serena
Campbell, California

MOCHA MOUSSE CRUNCH CAKE

10 servings

1 (16-ounce) family size Sara Lee Pound Cake, frozen, cut vertically into thin slices
2 tablespoons Amaretto liqueur or 1 teaspoon almond extract
2 tablespoons Kahlua liqueur or 1 tablespoon strong-brewed coffee mixed with 1 tablespoon chocolate sauce

Mousse Filling

1 package (2 tablespoons) unflavored gelatin
1/3 cup cold strong-brewed coffee
1 1/4 cups butter or margarine
1 (12-ounce) package semi-sweet chocolate chips
3/4 cup sugar
5 egg yolks
1 teaspoon vanilla extract
1 cup heavy cream
5 (1.4-ounce) chocolate-covered toffee candy bars, chopped

Chocolate Glaze

8 ounces semi-sweet chocolate, melted
1 tablespoon powdered sugar
1/3 cup strong-brewed coffee

Decoration

1/2 teaspoon unflavored gelatin
1 1/2 teaspoons water
1/2 cup heavy cream

Completely line an 8-inch round spring-form pan with plastic wrap or kitchen parchment; allow ends to fold out and over top of pan. Arrange about two-thirds of the Pound Cake slices over the bottom and around sides of pan, forming one even layer. Drizzle cake slices with liqueurs; set aside.

Mocha Mousse Crunch Cake recipe continued on page 12

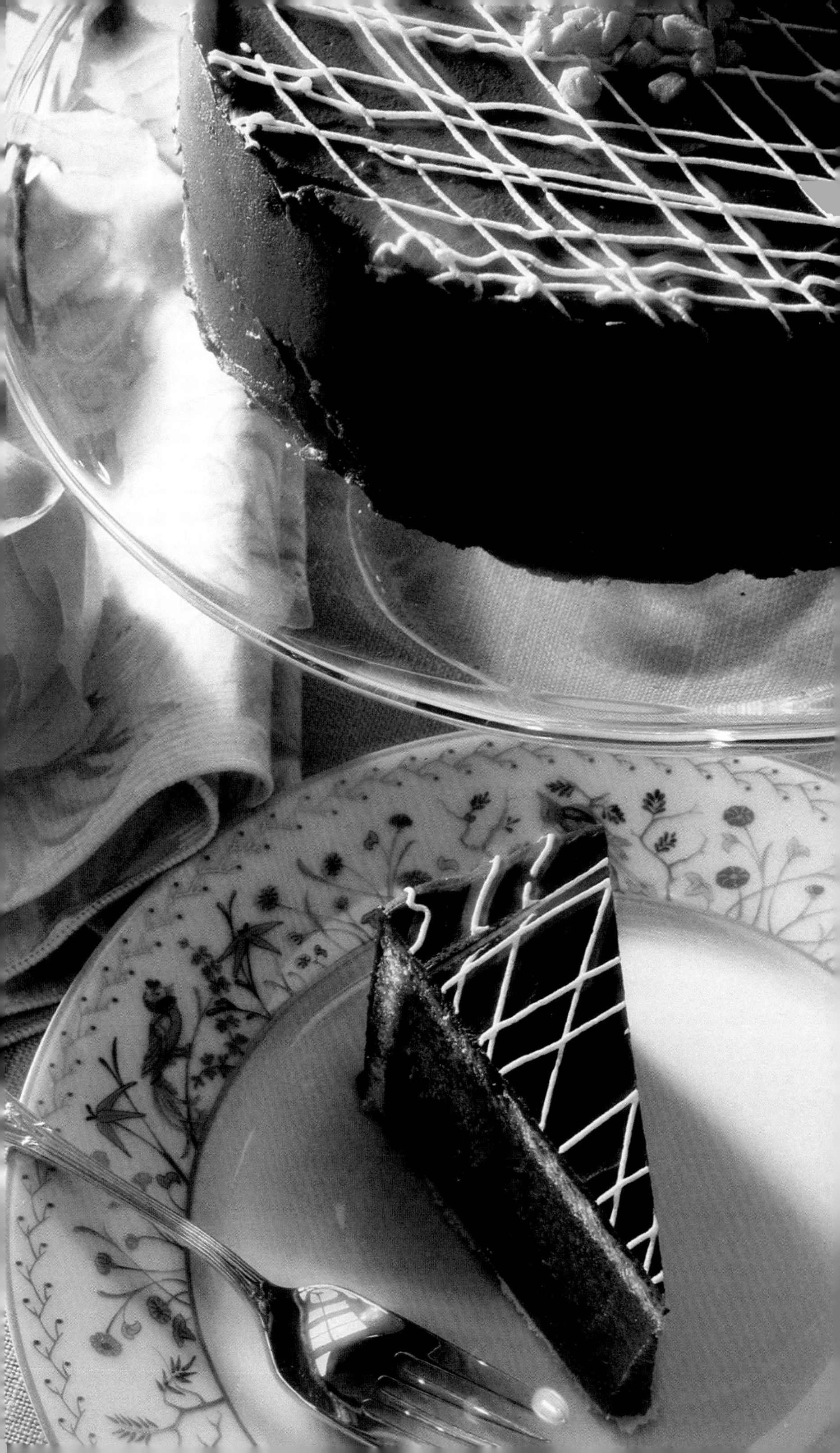

Mocha Mousse Crunch Cake recipe continued from page 10

To prepare mousse, sprinkle 2 tablespoons gelatin over cold coffee in a 1-cup measure. Allow gelatin to soften before stirring. In a large saucepan, melt butter over moderate heat; stir in coffee-gelatin mixture. Bring to a boil, stirring constantly. In a medium bowl, combine chocolate chips and sugar. Pour boiling coffee mixture over chocolate, stirring until smooth. Add egg yolks and vanilla, mixing well. Return to heat long enough to cook egg yolks, approximately 3 minutes, stirring constantly. Cool. In a chilled, deep, large bowl, beat cream with chilled beaters until stiff peaks form. Fold coffee-egg yolk mixture and 4 chopped candy bars into whipped cream.

Fill cake "shell" with mousse. Top mousse in "shell" with remaining Pound Cake slices. Cover last slice with plastic wrap and freeze until firm, about 4 hours.

To prepare chocolate glaze, combine chocolate and powdered sugar in a large bowl, mixing well. Gradually beat in coffee, until glaze is of smooth drizzling consistency; set aside. Remove cake from spring-form pan; slide cake onto a serving platter. Remove plastic wrap. Frost top and sides of cake with glaze.

To prepare cream decoration, dissolve gelatin in water in a small saucepan; stir over low heat until gelatin melts. Cool. In a chilled, large bowl, combine gelatin and cream; beat with chilled beaters until mixture forms stiff peaks.

To decorate, drizzle whipped cream from tips of a fork over cake. Or, using a pastry bag fitted with a number 1 tip, fill bag with whipped cream mixture and pipe a diamond pattern atop the cake. Garnish center of cake with remaining candy bar pieces.

Kim T. Happel
Louisville, Kentucky

Versatile Pound Cake Tips

Sara Lee received thousands of Pound Cake serving ideas from contest entrants. Here's a sample of suggestions from consumers.

Toast Pound Cake slices, then top with:

Sour cream, yogurt, or brown sugar

Sliced fresh or canned peaches, and fresh or frozen raspberries

Peanut butter and your favorite jelly or preserve

Scoop of chocolate or strawberry ice cream rolled in chopped nuts, topped with chocolate sauce

Brie cheese and sliced fresh pear

Cut Pound Cake into 3 horizontal layers; fill layers with:

Whipped cream blended with crushed peppermint candy

Prepared instant chocolate or vanilla-flavored pudding and pie filling mixed with fresh or canned fruit

Apple, blueberry, or cherry pie filling; top serving with dollop of whipped cream

Alternating layers of strawberry ice cream and sliced fresh strawberries

Peanut butter, finely chopped chocolate-covered toffee bars

Top plain Pound Cake slices with:

Sliced banana and prepared chocolate fudge sauce

Prepared instant chocolate-flavored pudding and pie filling blended with peanut butter

Whipped cream cheese mixed with mini chocolate chips and grated orange peel

Cheddar cheese slices and apple wedges

Applesauce blended with nutmeg or cinnamon

Cranberry sauce mixed with chopped pecans

SARA LEE CARAMEL CINNAMON HUTS

about 30 pieces

These little cakes are perfect to serve with tea or as a "little something" with after-dinner coffee.

1 (10 3/4-ounce) Sara Lee Pound Cake, frozen
1 1/2 cups sugar
1 tablespoon cinnamon
1 teaspoon allspice
1/2 teaspoon nutmeg
2 cups heavy cream
Powdered sugar to taste
Vanilla extract to taste
1/2 (3.4-ounce) package vanilla-flavored instant pudding and pie filling mix
1 cup caramel topping
2 tablespoons Kahlua liqueur or cold strong-brewed coffee
Additional caramel topping and cocoa for garnish

Cut Pound Cake vertically into 3/4-inch slices. Cut *each* slice into 3 equal pieces, then cut in half to form squares. In a large plastic food storage bag, combine sugar, cinnamon, allspice, and nutmeg; seal and shake to mix well. Add Pound Cake pieces, a few at a time; seal and shake to coat *each* piece well. Repeat until all cake pieces are coated with sugar-spice mixture; set aside. Reserve remaining mixture for garnish.

In a chilled, deep, medium bowl, beat cream with chilled beaters until soft peaks form; add powdered sugar and vanilla to taste. Continue to beat until stiff peaks form. Fold in instant vanilla pudding mix, caramel topping, and liqueur or coffee.

Arrange half the cake squares on a serving plate or tray. Fill a pastry bag fitted with a star tip with cream mixture; pipe cream onto *each* cake square on the serving plate. Top *each* with a second cake square, forming small "sandwiches". Decorate top of *each* with a rosette of cream filling. Garnish *each* with a drizzle of caramel topping, a sprinkle of cinnamon-sugar mixture, and a dusting of cocoa.

Linda Ervin
Landis, North Carolina

PEACH MELBA CLOUD

6 servings

A wonderful sweet to spruce up lunch or brunch occasions. If raspberries are unavailable, use fresh, sliced strawberries.

1 (10 3/4-ounce) Sara Lee Pound Cake, frozen
1/4 cup Amaretto liqueur
3/4 cup seedless red raspberry jam
2 cups heavy cream
1/2 (8-ounce) package cream cheese, softened
1/3 cup fruit cocktail, drained
1/3 cup peach schnapps liqueur
1 pint fresh raspberries

Cut Pound Cake into 6 horizontal layers. Cut two rounds from *each* layer with a glass or a biscuit cutter to make 12 rounds. (The rounds should be just slightly smaller in circumference than the parfait glasses used.)

In a small saucepan over moderate heat, melt Amaretto and jam together until smooth. Remove from heat and allow mixture to cool. Reserve 1/2 cup of mixture; set aside. Drizzle remaining mixture over cake rounds.

In a large, chilled, deep bowl, beat cream with chilled beaters until stiff. Add cream cheese and continue beating until well blended. Reserve 2 cups of this mixture in another bowl and set aside. To remaining cream mixture, blend in fruit cocktail and peach schnapps. Set aside. To the reserved cream cheese mixture, add remaining jam-Amaretto mixture and blend well.

Dollop fruit and cream mixture evenly in bottom of 6 parfait glasses; top with a Pound Cake round. Line inside rim of *each* glass with fresh raspberries. Using three fourths of jam and cream mixture, divide evenly among glasses, inside the fresh raspberry ring. Top this layer with another Pound Cake round.

Place remaining jam and cream mixture in a pastry bag fitted with an open star tip and pipe a decorative top on *each* dessert. Garnish with fresh raspberries. Refrigerate until ready to serve.

Vonnerie L. Wood
Marshall, Michigan

Amaretto Truffle Torte

8 servings

1 (10 3/4-ounce) Sara Lee Pound Cake, frozen

Almond Filling

1 cup almond paste
1 cup powdered sugar
1 cup cake or cookie crumbs
1 cup butter or margarine, softened
4 egg whites
1 or 2 tablespoons Amaretto liqueur

Chocolate Truffle Filling

1 (12-ounce) package semi-sweet chocolate chips
1 1/2 (8-ounce) packages cream cheese, softened
4 egg yolks
1/4 cup Amaretto liqueur

Almond Whipped Cream

1 cup heavy cream
1/4 cup powdered sugar
1/4 teaspoon almond extract

Slivered blanched almonds for garnish

Cut Pound Cake horizontally into 6 to 8 thin slices; set aside. In a medium bowl, combine the first 4 almond filling ingredients, mixing well. In a separate medium bowl, beat egg whites until stiff peaks form; carefully fold into almond mixture. Add Amaretto, a tablespoon at a time, until of desired spreading consistency; set aside. (See note)

In the top of a double boiler, melt chocolate chips over simmering water. In a medium bowl, beat cream cheese until smooth. Stir in chocolate. In a small bowl, beat egg yolks until frothy; add to chocolate-cheese mixture. Add Amaretto, beating well; set side.

Amaretto Truffle Torte recipe continued on page 20

Amaretto Truffle Torte recipe continued from page 18

Arrange one cake slice on a serving plate; evenly spread slice with almond filling (1/4 to 1/2 inch thick); top with a second slice and spread with chocolate filling (1/4 to 1/2 inch thick). Continue to "stack" cake slices and spread with fillings, alternating almond and then chocolate fillings, ending with a cake slice spread with chocolate filling. Spread three fourths of the remaining chocolate filling around the sides and top of the cake.

Fill a pastry bag fitted with a star-shaped tip with chocolate filling; pipe rosettes on the surface of the torte. Fill a second pastry bag fitted with a drop leaf tip with almond filling; pipe a dollop into the center of *each* rosette. Garnish with slivered almonds, if desired. Chill at least 4 hours before serving.

To prepare almond whipped cream, beat cream with chilled beaters in a chilled, deep, medium bowl until soft peaks form. Gradually add powdered sugar and almond extract; continue beating until stiff peaks form. To serve, cut torte into thin slices and garnish *each* portion with a dollop of almond-flavored whipped cream.

Note: This amount of filling makes enough for several cakes. Store, tightly covered, in refrigerator for up to 1 week.

Rita Reimer
Indialantic, Florida

2 SWEET REWARDS FOR EVERYDAY

Wouldn't it be great to have a delectable dessert after dinner, a little reward for all the effort you put in during the day that brings smiles to everyone around the table?

Sara Lee baked goods help you get out of the kitchen faster and still make a delicious dessert that tastes as good as it looks. All it takes is Sara Lee's versatile baked goods and a dash of creative flair. You don't have to be a culinary wizard or a kitchen genius.

Sara Lee Pound Cake is already prepared, so one major step is eliminated. Desserts on the following pages are easy to prepare and economical for everyday meals.

GOOEY CAKE

10 servings

For an attractive presentation, place a doily over top of cake. Using a strainer filled with powdered sugar, lightly dust cake by tapping on edge of strainer. Carefully remove doily to reveal lacey powdered sugar pattern underneath.

Preheat oven to 350°F.
Grease and flour a 10 1/4-inch round spring-form pan

1 (16-ounce) family size Sara Lee Pound Cake, thawed
1/4 cup unsalted butter or margarine, melted
2 eggs
2 (8-ounce) packages cream cheese, softened
1 (1-pound) package powdered sugar
1 teaspoon vanilla extract
1 pint *fresh* strawberries, stemmed and sliced, for garnish

Crumble Pound Cake into a food processor or blender container; cover and process or blend into fine crumbs. Add butter and 1 egg, blending well. Evenly spread mixture into pan.

In a medium bowl, combine remaining egg, cream cheese, powdered sugar, and vanilla; reserving 1/2 cup of powdered sugar; beat with an electric mixer at high speed for 2 minutes or until smooth. Spread over cake crumb layer in pan.

Bake 50 minutes or until browned. Cool; remove from pan and sprinkle with remaining powdered sugar. To serve, cut cake into wedges and garnish with chocolate sauce or *fresh* strawberries.

Colleen Muno
Chicago, Illinois

HANK'S FAVORITE ICE CREAM CAKE

8 servings

This is a big hit at children's parties!

1 (10 3/4-ounce) Sara Lee Pound Cake, frozen
1 quart chocolate chip mint-flavored ice cream or other favorite flavor, slightly softened
Prepared chocolate sauce, chocolate sprinkles, chopped walnuts, or sprigs of mint for garnishes (optional)

Horizontally cut 1/2-inch thick layer from top of Pound Cake; set aside. Hollow out the center of the remaining cake, being careful not to puncture the bottom of the cake (a soup spoon or grapefruit spoon works best). Crumble removed cake from the hollow. Place crumbs in a non-stick skillet and toast over moderate heat, stirring frequently, until golden brown. Cool and reserve.

Fill cake hollow with ice cream. Cover with reserved top layer of cake and gently press down. Frost top and sides with remaining ice cream. Cover with aluminum foil and freeze for at least 3 hours or up to one week before serving.

To serve, spoon chocolate sauce onto *each* of 8 dessert plates; place cake slices atop the sauce. Garnish with reserved crumbs, chocolate sprinkles, chopped walnuts, or sprigs of mint, if desired.

TUTTI FRUITTI YOGURT TRIFLE

8 servings

1 (10 3/4-ounce) Sara Lee Pound Cake, frozen
1 (3.4-ounce) package French vanilla-flavored instant pudding and pie filling mix
2 cups milk
2 medium bananas, peeled and thinly sliced
2 cups *fresh* or frozen blueberries
2 cups sliced *fresh* strawberries
3/4 cup pecans, chopped
2 cups frozen vanilla-flavored yogurt, slightly softened
Whole *fresh* strawberries for garnish

Cut Pound Cake into 1/2-inch thick cubes; toast in a toaster oven or broil on a baking sheet, 6 to 8 inches from heat source, until cake cubes are lightly browned, about 1 to 2 minutes. Line a deep 2 to 2 1/2-quart bowl (bottom and sides) with a layer of cake cubes fitted closely together.

Prepare pudding mix, adding milk according to package directions. Spoon pudding over cake cubes. Layer in order over pudding: sliced bananas, blueberries, and strawberries, sprinkling 1 tablespoon pecans between *each* layer. End with a layer of strawberries and evenly spread yogurt over top. Garnish with whole strawberries and remaining pecans. Serve immediately.

Note: Dessert can be prepared in advance, except for the yogurt layer, and refrigerated, covered, until ready to serve.

Hyacinth Rizzo
Snyder, New York

Quick Coconutty Chocolate Bars

24 bars

Preheat oven to 350°F.
Grease and flour a 13 x 9 x 2-inch baking pan

1 (10 3/4-ounce) Sara Lee Pound Cake, thawed
1/2 cup graham cracker crumbs (6 squares, crushed)
1/3 cup butter or margarine, melted
1/2 teaspoon vanilla extract
1 cup flaked coconut
1 cup semi-sweet chocolate chips
1/2 cup walnuts, coarsely chopped
1 (14-ounce) can sweetened condensed milk

Cut Pound Cake into small pieces. Combine cake pieces, graham cracker crumbs, butter, and vanilla in a food processor or blender container; cover and process or blend until mixture holds together. Evenly press cake mixture into the bottom of pan to form a crust.

In a medium bowl, combine coconut, chocolate chips, and nuts; evenly sprinkle mixture over crust. Drizzle condensed milk evenly over the coconut mixture in pan. Bake for 25 to 30 minutes or until done and lightly browned. Cool completely or chill before cutting into 24 bars.

Chocolate Pecan Stacks

4 servings

For a variation as shown in photo, a parfait glass or champagne flute may be used.

1 (10 3/4-ounce) Sara Lee Pound Cake, frozen
1 (8-ounce) package cream cheese, softened
2 cups milk
1 (3.4-ounce) package chocolate-flavored instant pudding and pie filling mix
1/2 cup finely chopped pecans

Cut Pound Cake horizontally into 4 equal-size layers. Place cake layers on a flat surface. Using a 3-inch diameter cookie or biscuit cutter or a glass with a 3-inch diameter rim, cut out 3 circles from *each* cake layer, for a total of 12 cake circles. Place remaining Pound Cake pieces in a blender or food processor container; cover and blend or process into crumbs. Set aside.

In a medium bowl, beat cream cheese at low speed of an electric mixer until smooth; add 1/2 cup milk, beating well. Add pudding mix and remaining milk; continue to beat for 2 minutes. Spoon a dollop of pudding into *each* of four 4-inch dessert bowls, spreading evenly.

Place a cake circle in *each* bowl, pressing down lightly into the pudding mixture. Cover *each* cake circle with another dollop of pudding, spreading evenly. Cover *each* with a second cake circle. Sprinkle *each* with chopped pecans. Top *each* with a third cake circle and then a dollop of pudding, spreading evenly. Refrigerate until ready to serve. Top *each* dessert with a sprinkle of Pound Cake crumbs.

Adam Manenti
Nyack, New York

POUND CAKE IN BOURBON ORANGE SAUCE

10 servings

When you need a quick dessert, this recipe goes together in minutes.

1 (10 3/4-ounce) Sara Lee Pound Cake, frozen
1 (12-ounce) jar apricot preserves
2 tablespoons orange juice
1 tablespoon bourbon whiskey
1 cup sliced *fresh* strawberries
1 teaspoon grated orange peel

Cut Pound Cake vertically into 10 slices. Place *each* slice on a flat surface and slice again diagonally in an "x" pattern, making 4 triangle-shaped pieces from *each* slice; set aside.

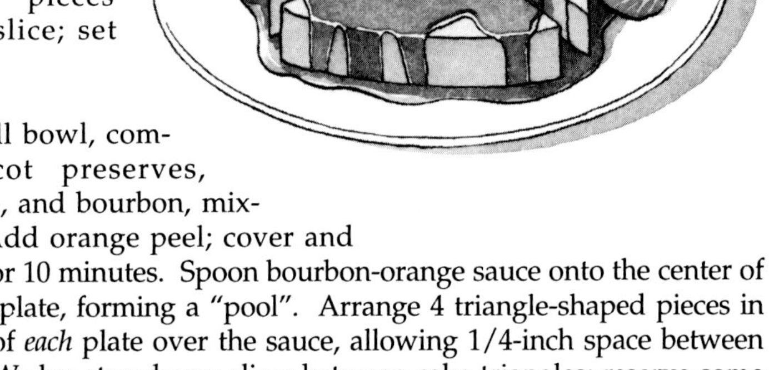

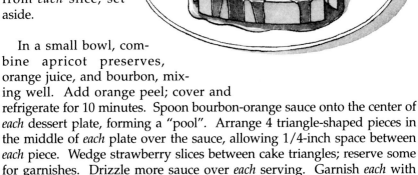

In a small bowl, combine apricot preserves, orange juice, and bourbon, mixing well. Add orange peel; cover and refrigerate for 10 minutes. Spoon bourbon-orange sauce onto the center of *each* dessert plate, forming a "pool". Arrange 4 triangle-shaped pieces in the middle of *each* plate over the sauce, allowing 1/4-inch space between *each* piece. Wedge strawberry slices between cake triangles; reserve some for garnishes. Drizzle more sauce over *each* serving. Garnish *each* with strawberry slices at both sides of *each* plate.

Helga Kajari
Vermillion, South Dakota

NEW AGE STRAWBERRY SHORTCAKE

10 servings

2 (10 3/4-ounce) Sara Lee Pound Cakes, frozen
1 (17-ounce) Sara Lee Original Cream Cheesecake, thawed
1 (16-ounce) container non-dairy whipped topping, thawed
1 pint *fresh* strawberries, stemmed and sliced
1/2 cup powdered sugar
Additional whole *fresh* strawberries for garnish

Cut *each* Pound Cake vertically into 10 equal-size slices, making 20 total slices.

In a food processor or blender, combine Cheesecake and half of the non-dairy whipped topping. Cover and process or blend until smooth. Set aside.

Coat inside of medium bowl with non-stick vegetable oil cooking spray. Press Pound Cake slices in one layer over bottom and up sides of bowl to form a cake "shell". Spread a layer of Cheesecake filling over Pound Cake; cover with sliced strawberries and another layer of Pound Cake. Repeat layering procedure until bowl is filled to top, ending with a Pound Cake layer. Refrigerate at least 6 hours.

Invert bowl onto a cake plate; gently loosen dessert from bowl onto the plate. To frost, combine remaining whipped topping and powdered sugar, mixing lightly. Frost cake and garnish with additional whole strawberries.

Gloria Guerra
Chicago, Illinois

Blueberry Cheesecake

6 servings

Preheat oven to 325°F.
Grease a 9 x 9 x 2-inch baking pan

1 (10 3/4-ounce) Sara Lee Pound Cake, frozen
2 (8-ounce) packages cream cheese, softened
2 eggs
2/3 cup sugar
1 teaspoon vanilla extract
1 teaspoon lemon juice
1 (15 1/4 to 16 3/4-ounce) can blueberry pie filling

Cut Pound Cake vertically into 12 equal-size slices. Arrange cake slices in pan. Where necessary, cut pieces to fill in any gaps. In a medium bowl, beat cream cheese until smooth; add eggs, sugar, vanilla, and lemon juice, mixing well. Spoon mixture over cake slices, spreading evenly. Bake for 1 hour or until a knife inserted in the middle comes out clean. Remove from oven and cool completely. Place a piece of wax paper over top of cake and invert onto a plate; then invert again onto a serving plate (the cake will be turned right-side up). Spoon blueberry filling over Cheesecake and serve.

Donna Gish
Blue Springs, Missouri

Upside Down Cheesecake

10 servings

Line an 8 1/2 x 4 1/2 x 2 1/2-inch loaf pan with wax paper

1 (10 3/4-ounce) Sara Lee Pound Cake, frozen
1 (16-ounce) package frozen sliced strawberries, thawed, drained (reserve 1/3 cup juice)
1 (8-ounce) package cream cheese, softened
1 cup prepared lemon pie filling
2 teaspoons powdered sugar
1/2 teaspoon lemon juice

Frosting
1 cup heavy cream
Sugar and vanilla extract to taste

Cut Pound Cake vertically into 10 even slices. Arrange cake slices over bottom of pan, crumbling some to fill any openings. Press into place and drizzle with reserved strawberry juice. In a medium bowl, beat cream cheese until smooth; add lemon filling, powdered sugar, and lemon juice, mixing well. Evenly spread filling over cake layer; cover filling with remaining cake slices. Cover with wax paper and refrigerate for at least 4 hours.

To prepare whipped cream frosting, beat cream with chilled beaters in a chilled, deep, medium bowl until stiff peaks form. Add sugar and vanilla to taste.

To serve, invert cake onto a serving platter and gently remove cake from pan. Frost with whipped cream. Slice and serve with remaining strawberries. If cake is not frosted, top *each* slice with 2 tablespoons berries.

Mary Anne League
Sutherlin, Oregon

ANGEL PUDDING

10 to 12 servings

1 (10 3/4-ounce) Sara Lee Pound Cake, frozen
1 cup cold milk
1 teaspoon rum extract or flavoring
1 (3.4-ounce) package vanilla-flavored instant pudding and pie filling mix
1/2 cup heavy cream
1 (11-ounce) can mandarin orange sections, drained
1 cup sliced *fresh* or frozen strawberries or whole raspberries
1 cup shredded coconut

Cut Pound Cake horizontally into 3 equal-size layers; cut *each* layer into 1-inch cubes. Place in a large bowl. In a 1-cup measure, combine 1/4 cup milk and rum extract; drizzle over cake cubes, tossing lightly. Prepare pudding according to package directions, using only 3/4 cup milk; spoon over cake cubes. In a chilled, deep, small bowl, beat cream with chilled beaters until stiff peaks form. Fold whipped cream, oranges, and berries into cake-pudding mixture. Cover and refrigerate at least 3 hours before serving. Dessert may be prepared up to 3 days in advance. To serve, spoon into dessert bowls and top *each* with shredded coconut.

Another Recipe From:
Mary Anne League
Sutherlin, Oregon

STRAWBERRY BANANA COPA CABANA SPLIT

8 servings

For a variation, as shown in picture: leave the top off and serve open face, garnished with strawberries and granola.

1 (10 3/4-ounce) Sara Lee Pound Cake, frozen
1 large banana, peeled
1 cup granola
1/2 cup chocolate sauce
1 (8-ounce) container frozen yogurt, flavor of your choice, slightly softened
1 cup sliced *fresh* strawberries for garnish

Horizontally cut 1/2-inch thick layer from top of Pound Cake; reserve and set aside. Hollow out bottom center of Pound Cake with a grapefruit or soup spoon, leaving about 1/2-inch thick layer in bottom of hollow. Place on a serving platter. Crumble scooped-out cake into crumbs for garnish; set aside. Lay the banana lengthwise in the hollow.

In a small bowl, combine granola and chocolate sauce; spread mixture around and over the banana. Replace the top layer of Pound Cake, gently pressing down. Frost with yogurt. Freeze 2 hours before serving. Garnish with sliced strawberries and Pound Cake crumbs before serving.

C.W. Brantman
Minneapolis, Minnesota

PIE POSSIBILITIES

Sara Lee makes pie possible anytime. All you do is take a Sara Lee Pie out of the freezer and pop it into the oven. Here are a few ideas to make this truly American dessert an even more enjoyable treat:

Before placing in the oven, rub pie crust with milk; it will produce a glossy, golden brown crust.

Peach or Apple Pie: While still hot from the oven, spread apricot preserves over the top; sprinkle with grated nuts and coconut.

Cherry Pie: While still hot from the oven, grate semi-sweet chocolate over the top.

Apple Pie: Sprinkle grated Cheddar, or place strips of Brie cheese over the top of pie during final 10 minutes of baking.

When pie is cool from oven, remove from pie tin and turn upside down on a baking sheet. Frost with meringue and place under the broiler for 5 minutes or until peaks are browned.

Tips to use that one piece of left-over pie

Crumble over ice cream for a topping, or break up pie and serve topped with ice cream like a cobbler.

Apple Pie: Break up into an oven-proof dessert dish; cover with grated cheese and raisins. Microwave or pop under the broiler until cheese melts.

Cherry or Peach Pie: Layer into parfait glasses with ice cream or *fresh* sliced fruit.

Speedy Sauces to Liven up Favorite Pies

VANILLA SAUCE FOR APPLE PIE

1 cup milk
1 cup heavy cream
1/2 cup sugar
2 teaspoons vanilla extract
3 egg yolks
Nutmeg or cinnamon for garnish

Bring all ingredients, except yolks, to a boil in a medium saucepan. Reduce heat and simmer for 10 minutes. In a bowl, whisk egg yolks until foamy. Stir yolks into sauce mixture and continue to heat until foam starts to appear around edge of pan. Remove from heat and cool to room temperature. Spoon onto center of dessert plate; place pie slice on top of sauce. Garnish with sprinkle of nutmeg or cinnamon.

APRICOT RUM SAUCE FOR PEACH PIE

1 1/2 cups sugar
3 (12-ounce) jars apricot jam (no-sugar-added) or spreadable fruit
3/4 cup rum
3 teaspoons *fresh* lemon juice

In a small saucepan, combine sugar, jam, and rum; bring to a rapid boil for 5 minutes. Remove from heat and stir in lemon juice. Spoon over pie slices.

CHOCOLATE STRAWBERRY VANILLA SAUCE FOR CHERRY PIE

1 (12-ounce) package mini semi-sweet chocolate chips
1 cup frozen strawberries, thawed, include juice
2 teaspoons vanilla extract
Grand Marnier liqueur to taste

Combine all ingredients, except Grand Marnier, in a food processor or blender container; cover and process or blend until smooth. Gradually add Grand Marnier and continue processing or blending until sauce consistency. Generously spoon onto center of dessert plates and top with a pie slice.

FLAVORED WHIPPED CREAM

Pie dolloped with whipped cream is a welcome combination. The secret to fluffy, irresistible white clouds of cream is chilling both beaters and bowl. Beat 1 cup heavy cream, starting at low speed of an electric mixer. When cream begins to thicken, add 1/2 teaspoon vanilla extract and powdered sugar to taste and switch to high speed. Just before peaks begin to form, add 1 tablespoon of your favorite flavoring and continue beating until stiff, but creamy. Here are several tasty options: Chocolate, Coffee, Cointreau, or Grand Marnier liqueur, or Peach Schnapps, Apple Brandy, or Calvados, or your favorite fruit juice.

CANNOLI SQUARES

10 servings

For a taste variation, substitute halved Macadamia nuts or whole blanched almonds for pistachios.

1 (10 3/4-ounce) Sara Lee Pound Cake, frozen
8 ounces ricotta cheese
2 tablespoons powdered sugar
1 (6-ounce) package pistachio nuts, shelled
1 (12-ounce) package semi-sweet chocolate chips

Cut Pound Cake vertically into 10 equal-size slices; set aside. In a medium bowl, beat cheese with powdered sugar until smooth.

Place cake slices on a flat surface; spread a thin layer of the cheese mixture over *each* slice. Cut *each* in half vertically, making 20 squares. Decorate half of *each* cake square with chocolate chips. Decorate remaining half of *each* with pistachio nuts. Serve 2 squares per person.

3 When Only the Best Will Do

There's nothing quite as pleasing to the eye or palate as a beautiful, luscious dessert to top off an elegant dinner party or family event. When guests are coming for dinner and there's no time to cook, you need a dessert that will look good and taste wonderful while taking minimal effort to prepare.

Sara Lee baked goods are in your freezer, right there when you need them most, ready for special occasions and dessert emergencies. With a little extra touch, Sara Lee Pound Cake, Cheesecake, Layer Cake, and Pie can be dressed up to suit any dessert occasion. Sara Lee Pound Cake has a soft, moist texture that creates all kinds of possibilities for cutting, molding, shaping, building, and making beautiful, delightful desserts that look like you slaved in the kitchen for days. The good news: You didn't.

These desserts look like they came from the corner bakery, but you made them yourself quickly and economically, too.

Bon Appetit!

DIXIE PEACH & KIWI TRIFLE

10 servings

No-bake convenience! This cake is so attractive, it can be used as a centerpiece for a dinner or buffet table.

3 (10 3/4-ounce) Sara Lee Pound Cakes, frozen
1 (3.4-ounce) vanilla-flavored instant pudding and pie filling mix
2 cups milk
1 (12-ounce) jar peach preserves
1/2 cup apple juice
6 firm ripe kiwi, peeled
2 (16-ounce) cans peach halves, drained (see note)
Sprigs of *fresh* mint for garnish

Cut *each* Pound Cake horizontally into 4 equal-size layers. Place 2 layers side-by-side in the bottom of a 9-inch round spring-form pan. Cut pieces from a third layer to fill in the gaps, making a round layer of cake. Press the pieces together with finger tips. Reserve remaining cake.

In a medium bowl, combine pudding mix and milk; beat at low speed of an electric mixer for 2 minutes. Set aside. In a separate small bowl, combine peach preserves and apple juice; stir vigorously with a fork until blended. Set aside. Slice kiwi into 1/4-inch thick circles; set aside. Cut *each* peach half into 4 or 5 slices; set aside.

To assemble trifle, spread cake layer in pan liberally with peach preserves mixture. Evenly spread half of the vanilla pudding over the glazed cake layer. Place another layer of cake (done the same way as the first) over the pudding in pan; liberally spread with peach preserves mixture. Arrange a layer of kiwi and peach slices over second cake layer. Overlap kiwi slices around the outside edge of the layer; fill the center of the layer with peach slices. Spread peach preserves mixture over fruit.

Repeat another layer of cake, glaze evenly with preserves, and cover with remaining pudding. Top with another layer of cake. Spread top cake layer with preserves mixture and arrange fruit as described before. Brush fruit with remaining peach preserves mixture. Chill in the refrigerator for at least 2 hours to set before serving.

To serve, carefully remove spring-form; cut cake trifle into wedges, arrange on dessert plates, and garnish *each* serving with a *fresh* mint sprig.

Note: Sliced canned peaches are too thick. Six *fresh* peaches, blanched, pitted, and peeled, may be substituted for canned peaches; cut *each* in half and slice as previously directed. This dessert may be prepared and refrigerated for up to 2 days before serving.

CHOCOLATE RASPBERRY DOBOSCH TORTE

8 servings

One of our favorites as photographed on the cover.

1 (10 3/4-ounce) Sara Lee Pound Cake, frozen
2 (8-ounce) containers prepared chocolate frosting
1 (12-ounce) container seedless raspberry jam
24 whole toasted almonds for garnish

Cut Pound Cake horizontally into 4 equal-size layers. Place a layer on a serving platter. Frost with chocolate; top with another cake layer and spread with jam. Frost third cake layer with chocolate; cover with fourth cake layer and frost Pound Cake on all sides with remaining chocolate frosting. Decorate top of cake with whole, toasted almonds. Cut Pound Cake into 8 vertical slices and serve.

Note: To toast almonds, see page 44.

BERRY MOUSSE CAKE

8 servings

1/4 cup evaporated skim milk
1 (10 3/4-ounce) Sara Lee Pound Cake, frozen
1 envelope (2 tablespoons) unflavored gelatin
3/4 cup apple juice
1 (10-ounce) package frozen strawberries or raspberries, thawed and drained (juice reserved)
1 egg white
1 teaspoon Grand Marnier liqueur or orange juice
Fresh berries, mint sprigs, or chocolate shavings, as desired, for garnish

Pour milk into a deep, medium bowl; chill milk, bowl, and beaters in freezer for 3 minutes.

Place Pound Cake top-side down centered on a serving plate. With a knife, trace a 5 1/2 x 2-inch rectangle centered on top of cake. Hollow out this area of cake using a grapefruit or soup spoon, leaving a thin bottom layer in the hollow. Place scooped-out cake in a non-stick medium skillet; crumble with a fork and brown over moderate heat. Cool and set aside.

In a small saucepan, dissolve gelatin in apple juice and stir over low heat for 1 minute. Transfer mixture to a large bowl and cool. Add egg white, reserved berry juice, and Grand Marnier to liquified gelatin; mix well. Place in the freezer for 30 minutes.

Place berries in a blender container or food processor; cover and blend or process until puréed. Strain to remove seeds; set aside. Beat chilled berry mixture at high speed of an electric mixer until mixture doubles in bulk; fold in puréed berries. Beat chilled milk with chilled beaters until milk forms stiff peaks; fold into fruit mixture.

To assemble cake, spoon mousse mixture into cake hollow, filling to the top and forming a rounded mound. (Because mousse contains a large amount of air, it will settle before serving.) Frost sides and top of cake with mousse; reserve remaining mousse. Sprinkle toasted crumbs over top and sides of the cake. Chill cake and remaining mousse, uncovered for 4 hours, or until mousse is firm.

To serve, cut cake into slices; surround *each* serving with additional mousse and garnish with berries, a mint sprig, or chocolate shavings. Serve immediately.

Chocolate Imperial Cheesecake

6 servings

1 (17-ounce) Sara Lee Original Cream Cheesecake, frozen
1/2 cup dipping semi-sweet or bittersweet chocolate (see note)
1/2 cup dipping milk chocolate (see note)
Semi-sweet chocolate chips for garnish (optional)

Remove Cheesecake from foil pan and place on a serving plate; allow to thaw completely. Place dipping chocolates in separate bowls; cover loosely and microwave at high power for 40 seconds. Coat the tines of a fork in semi-sweet or bittersweet chocolate; drizzle chocolate from the fork tines over the cake, creating an abstract stripe pattern. Repeat in opposite direction, drizzling milk chocolate over the semi-sweet or bittersweet chocolate. To garnish sprinkle *each* serving with chocolate chips, if desired.

Note: Dipping chocolate is available at most supermarkets. It usually comes in microwave-safe jars and is a quick way to make many ordinary items special.

Toffee Crunch Cake

8 to 10 servings

Toffee fans will love the caramel flavor and crunchy, creamy texture.

1 (10 3/4-ounce) Sara Lee Pound Cake, frozen
2 cups heavy cream
3/4 cup butterscotch syrup
3 (1.4-ounce) chocolate-covered toffee candy bars, coarsely chopped

Cut Pound Cake horizontally into 3 equal-size layers; set aside. In a chilled, large, deep bowl, beat cream with chilled beaters until stiff peaks form. Gradually add butterscotch syrup, folding in gently. Place a cake layer on a serving plate. Liberally frost with whipped cream mixture. Sprinkle layer with one-third of the candy bars. Arrange a second cake layer over the first layer and repeat process. Top with the third cake layer. Frost top and sides of cake with remaining whipped cream mixture.

Drizzle remaining butterscotch syrup over cake. Sprinkle remaining candy bars over cake. Chill in refrigerator for at least 3 hours before serving.

Variations: Use strawberry or chocolate syrup in place of butterscotch syrup and garnish with chopped frozen strawberries or semi-sweet chocolate chips.

Ann Fowler
Lowville, New York

CREAMY TORTE

8 servings

1 (10 3/4-ounce) Sara Lee Pound Cake, frozen

Filling

8 ounces ricotta cheese
2 ounces milk chocolate, grated
2 tablespoons powdered sugar
2 tablespoons toasted blanched almonds (see note)
1/8 teaspoon cinnamon
1/4 cup chopped maraschino cherries, dark seedless raisins, or chopped dried apricots

Frosting

1 (8-ounce) container non-dairy whipped topping, thawed
1/2 cup powdered sugar
1/2 teaspoon almond extract

Additional toasted blanched almonds for garnish.

Cut Pound Cake horizontally into 3 equal-size layers; set aside. To prepare filling, process cheese in a food processor or blender, covered, for 60 seconds or until smooth. Add milk chocolate, powdered sugar, almonds, and cinnamon; cover and process for 30 seconds. Fold in cherries by hand.

To assemble cake, place a cake layer on a serving plate; spread with half of the filling. Top with a second cake layer and spread with remaining filling. Place the third cake layer atop the filling; set aside.

To prepare frosting, combine non-dairy whipped topping and powdered sugar together in a medium bowl. Add almond extract and beat until smooth. Frost top and sides of the cake. Garnish with toasted almonds. Chill several hours before serving.

Note: To toast almonds, spread whole blanched almonds in one layer over an ungreased baking sheet; bake in a preheated slow oven (325°F.) for 8 to 10 minutes or until almonds are lightly browned.

Jan Weaver
Aberdeen, South Dakota

Cocoa Almond Cheesecake

6 servings

1 (17-ounce) Sara Lee Original Cream Cheesecake, frozen
1/2 cup sliced blanched almonds
1/4 cup cocoa powder

Remove Cheesecake from foil container and place on a sheet of wax paper; thaw for 10 minutes. Sprinkle almond slices evenly over cake, patting down gently with finger tips. Place cocoa powder in a small strainer. Using sheets of paper as templates, create three even stripes of cocoa dust atop the cake. To make the first stripe, cover two-thirds of the cake with a sheet of paper, leaving the outer edge (approximately 1 1/2 inches at widest point) exposed. Place strainer over exposed edge and tap rim lightly to dust cake.

To make the middle stripe, use two sheets of paper to cover the outer thirds of the cake, leaving the middle exposed. Repeat cocoa dusting. Repeat template procedure for outer edge on opposite side of cake and dust with cocoa. Using two large pancake spatulas, carefully transfer cake to a serving plate.

Petite Chocolate Raspberry Cakes

4 servings

These cakes look like fine European pastry. Serve as an elegant conclusion to your dinner party with espresso-style coffee.

1 (10 3/4-ounce) Sara Lee Pound Cake, frozen
1 (8-ounce) jar seedless red raspberry jam

Chocolate Icing

1 (12-ounce) package semi-sweet chocolate chips
1/2 cup heavy cream
6 tablespoons Amaretto or other almond liqueur
3 tablespoons unsalted butter or margarine

1 cup sliced almonds

Raspberry Sauce

2 cups *fresh* or frozen raspberries (see note)
1/2 cup sugar
1/4 cup water

***Fresh* raspberries for decoration (see note)**

Cut Pound Cake horizontally into 2 equal-size halves. Leaving the two halves on top of *each* other, vertically cut into 4 equal-size slices. Round off the corners and place on a wire rack or wax paper. Spread raspberry jam evenly between and on top of the slices; set aside.

To prepare icing, combine all ingredients in a medium saucepan; stir over low heat until chocolate mixture is melted and smooth. Cool. Cover and refrigerate until icing is chilled. To frost cakes, spread icing over *each* cake, fully coating top and sides. Allow cakes to stand about 15 minutes. Decorate *each* cake with almond slices and *fresh* raspberries. Refrigerate cakes for 1 hour or until chocolate is firm.

To prepare raspberry sauce, combine all ingredients in a small saucepan; cook over moderate heat until mixture is reduced by one-third, about 15 minutes. Strain sauce to remove seeds. Cool thoroughly.

To serve, spoon raspberry sauce onto the center of *each* of 4 dessert plates. Arrange a decorated cake in the center of *each* plate.

Note: If raspberries are unavailable, strawberries may be substituted.

Alec Adams
Ogunquit, Maine

STUFFED POUND PUDDING

8 servings

This is an anytime favorite that can also be served warmed-up for breakfast.

Preheat oven to 350°F.
Grease and flour a 9 x 5 x 3-inch loaf pan

1 (10 3/4-ounce) Sara Lee Pound Cake, frozen
1 quart (4 cups) half & half
4 egg yolks
4 eggs
1/4 cup sugar
1/2 teaspoon vanilla extract
4 ounces dried apricots
2 prunes, pitted
1 seedless medium orange, peeled and quartered
1/3 cup pecans, chopped
1 tablespoon Cointreau liqueur or orange juice
1 tablespoon honey

Orange Sauce

1 (12-ounce) jar orange marmalade
2 tablespoons orange juice
2 teaspoons grated orange peel
1 teaspoon Cointreau liqueur or orange juice

Cut Pound Cake horizontally into 3 equal-size layers. Cut a piece of kitchen parchment paper to cover the bottom of loaf pan; grease paper and fit into the pan. Arrange one cake layer in the pan. Cut the remaining cake into 1/2-inch cubes; place in a medium bowl and set aside.

In a large bowl, combine egg yolks, eggs, sugar, and vanilla, mixing well. Add half & half, 1/2 cup at a time, mixing until sugar is dissolved. Pour mixture over cake cubes and allow to soak for 15 minutes.

Combine apricots, prunes, and orange in a food processor or blender container; cover and process or blend until the mixture becomes a paste. Transfer to a small bowl and stir in pecans, Cointreau, and honey. Spread apricot mixture over cake layer in pan. Cover layer with soaked cake cubes and any remaining liquid.

Bake for 1 hour. Cool before removing from pan. To prepare orange sauce, combine all ingredients in a small bowl, blending well with a wire whisk or fork. To serve, cut into slices and spoon orange sauce over *each* serving.

Marlene Steinberg
Marina Del Rey, California

CHEESECAKE ISABELLA

6 servings

1 (26-ounce) Sara Lee Strawberry French Cheesecake, thawed
1 (17-ounce) package Sara Lee Original Cream Cheesecake, thawed
2 drops red food coloring
1/2 cup sliced *fresh* strawberries for garnish

Cut Strawberry French Cheesecake into pieces. Place in a food processor or blender container; add food coloring, cover, and purée until smooth. Spray the inside of a 5-cup heart or ring mold with non-stick vegetable oil cooking spray. Spoon Cheesecake mixture into bottom of the mold; freeze until firm.

Cut Original Cream Cheesecake into pieces. Place in a food processor or blender container; cover and purée until smooth. Spoon over the frozen Cheesecake, spreading evenly. Cover with plastic wrap and freeze for at least 6 hours. When ready to serve, turn out Cheesecake onto serving platter; garnish with *fresh* strawberries.

Note: To unmold the Cheesecake easily, dip bottom of mold in warm water for 30 seconds.

Isabella Buchanan
Issaquah, Washington

WEDDING CAKE

150 servings

Here are eleven easy steps to a quick, affordable, delicious no-bake wedding cake.

The assembly time is approximately one hour. Each Sara Lee Pound Cake (10 3/4-ounce) provides 10 servings. To determine size of the cake, divide the number of guests by 10 which will determine the number of Sara Lee Pound Cakes to use and the size of the wedding cake. Since Sara Lee Pound Cakes are rectangular in shape, a square wedding cake is the easiest shape to assemble.

For example: To serve 150 guests with a four-tier cake, 15 cakes are used — 8 for the bottom layer, 4 1/2 for the second layer, 2 for the third layer and 1/2 for the top. For a larger wedding, 21 cakes are used to serve 210 guests with a three-tier cake: 12 for the bottom layer, 6 for the second layer, and 3 for the top.

Keep Pound Cakes frozen until ready to assemble. Frozen cakes are easier to frost and do not shed crumbs.

To save time, use prepared, vanilla-flavored cake frosting. Or, use a homemade buttercream or powdered sugar icing, if desired. Boiled frostings do not hold well.

The top 2 layers may be sprinkled liberally with Grand Marnier liqueur, if desired, before frosting.

Use imagination and the couple's preferences for a guide. If chocolate is their favorite flavor, use as a center filling. Or, frost the outside with chocolate frosting and spread the cake layers with peanut butter and sprinkle with crushed peanut butter candies.

Use a wide rubber spatula to frost the cake. A pastry bag is not necessary for decorations. Silk flowers, ribbons, or pearls can be used. A special decoration should be placed on the top layer which the bridal couple will keep, freeze, and enjoy together on their first anniversary. A keepsake bridal couple in ceramic or a pair of wedding bells are traditional.

Wedding Cake recipe continued on page 52

Wedding Cake recipe continued from page 50

Ingredients

1 sheet of 1/2-inch plywood cut to exact size of finished cake, 16-inches square, covered with aluminum foil
15 (10 3/4-ounce) Sara Lee Pound Cakes, frozen
4 cups seedless red raspberry jam or spreadable fruit
4 cups unsalted walnuts, ground
6 1/4 cups favorite white frosting
4 straight candy canes
1 (200-square foot) roll aluminum foil
4 column cake separators (optional), layers can be set on-top of each other
Silk flowers, ribbons, or pearls for decoration

To assemble cake:

1. Cover board with foil.
2. Stack Pound Cakes while still in boxes and make a plan for decoration scheme.
3. Remove cakes from boxes; save cardboard lids from all cakes. Assemble bottom square tier on board, using 8 cakes.
4. Cut *each* cake in half horizontally and spread the bottom half of *each* with jam; sprinkle *each* with nuts. Replace the top half of *each*. Frost around the sides and top of assembled cake square, making one large bottom cake tier.
5. Assemble second tier using 4 1/2 cakes. Repeat step 4 to form second tier.
6. After top of second tier is frosted, gently press the 4 candy canes into the second tier in the exact location of the columns. They will give the columns added support. Gently place columns on second tier and press into frosting.
7. Make the support for the third tier by cross-hatching the cardboard tops from the Sara Lee Cakes boxes. Stack 3 lids on top of *each* other; repeat with 3 more immediately next to them. Wrap this "lid platform" tightly in aluminum foil. Repeat the process for a second layer and place the wrapped layer vertically — cross-hatched — over the first layer; wrap the two together tightly with aluminum foil. Repeat for a third layer. Place the "lid platform" on top of the columns.
8. Assemble third tier, using 2 cakes. Repeat step 4.
9. Assemble top tier, using 1/2 cake. Repeat step 4.
10. Touch-up frosting overall. If a smooth affect is desired, dip a rubber spatula in water and gently move the side of it in one direction over the frosting. Remove any excess frosting the spatula has "dragged" with it.
11. Decorate with silk flowers, ribbons, pearls, etc. Wash decorations in mild soap and dry thoroughly before using. Be sure to wrap with aluminum foil anything that will be inserted into cake, except the candy canes.

TRUFFLE BERRY CAKE

6 to 8 servings

1 (10 3/4-ounce) Sara Lee Pound Cake, frozen
7 tablespoons Chocolate Truffle liqueur or chocolate sauce
1 cup heavy cream
1 (10-ounce) package frozen blackberries, thawed and drained (see note)
Grated bittersweet or semi-sweet chocolate for garnish

Cut Pound Cake horizontally into 3 equal-size layers. Arrange cake layers on a flat surface; pierce *each* all over with a fork. Drizzle 2 tablespoons liqueur over *each* layer, filling pierced holes.

In a chilled, small bowl, beat cream with chilled beaters until stiff peaks form. Add remaining 1 tablespoon liqueur to whipped cream, folding gently.

Place one cake layer on a serving plate and spread with a thin layer of whipped cream. Cover whipped cream with berries. Place another cake layer over berries and repeat. Finish with third Pound Cake layer. Frost top and sides of cake with remaining whipped cream. Refrigerate at least 2 hours before serving. Evenly sprinkle top of cake with grated chocolate.

Note: Cut 37 partially frozen berries in half lengthwise for filling and reserve whole berries for garnish. Place blackberry halves, rounded-side up on cake layers over whipped cream filling.

Margo Scofield
Fair Oaks, California

PINK CLOUD CAKE

8 servings

This light, airy cake is picture-perfect to serve at a luncheon or shower.

2 (10 3/4-ounce) Sara Lee Pound Cakes, frozen
1 1/2 to 2 cups *fresh* strawberries or raspberries, stemmed
1 tablespoon powdered sugar
1 cup heavy cream
1/2 cup sugar
1/4 teaspoon vanilla extract
3 egg whites
Sprigs of mint for garnish

Cut *each* Pound Cake horizontally into 4 equal-size layers making a total of 8 layers. Coat the inside of 9 x 5 x 3-inch loaf pan with non-stick vegetable oil cooking spray. Arrange a cake layer in bottom of pan. Cut pieces from remaining slices to fill gaps so all layers are solid. Press pieces together with fingers; set aside.

In a medium bowl, combine 3/4 cup berries with powdered sugar; set aside. Place remaining berries in a food processor or blender container; cover and purée. In a chilled, large bowl, beat cream with chilled beaters at high speed of an electric mixer for 30 seconds. Add sugar and vanilla; continue beating until stiff peaks form. Fold berry purée into whipped cream. In a deep, medium bowl, beat egg whites at high speed of an electric mixer until stiff peaks form; fold into berry mixture. Cover and refrigerate until chilled.

Evenly spread a layer of raspberry mousse mixture over cake layer in pan. Top mousse with second cake layer, being careful to fill gaps with additional cake pieces. Cover cake layer with sweetened berries. Place a third cake layer over berries. Spoon another layer of mousse over third cake layer. Top mousse layer with final cake layer. Cover cake and refrigerate for 3 hours. Loosely cover and reserve remaining mousse in refrigerator.

Invert loaf pan over serving plate; tap sides with fingers and shake lightly until cake releases. Frost cake with reserved raspberry mousse. Chill until ready to serve. Cut into slices and garnish individual servings with reserved *fresh* berries and/or sprigs of mint.

TIRAMISU

5 servings

Great as a finale
to your favorite pasta.

1 (10 3/4-ounce) Sara Lee Pound Cake, frozen
1/4 cup strong-brewed coffee
1 (16-ounce) container non-dairy whipped topping, thawed
1/2 cup sweetened cocoa powder

Cut Pound Cake vertically into 10 equal-size slices. Drizzle coffee over *each* slice; set aside.

In a large bowl, combine whipped topping and 1/4 cup cocoa, mixing until blended. Place 5 cake slices on a flat surface. Evenly spread a thick layer of whipped topping mixture over *each* slice. Top *each* with a second cake slice, sandwich-style. Transfer to individual dessert plates. Spread *each* cake "sandwich" with whipped topping mixture. Cut "sandwiches" diagonally in half. Sprinkle with remaining cocoa; serve immediately.

POUND CAKE WITH PEAR SAUCE AND RASPBERRY PURÉE

10 servings

Preheat oven to 350°F.

1 (10 3/4-ounce) Sara Lee Pound Cake, frozen
2 tablespoons light brown sugar
1 teaspoon cinnamon
2 firm, medium to large pears, peeled and cored
1/2 cup apple juice
1 tablespoon flour
1 (10-ounce) package frozen raspberries, thawed
1 tablespoon orange juice
1 1/2 teaspoons powdered sugar
Whole *fresh* raspberries, mint sprigs, or orange slices for garnish

Cut Pound Cake vertically into 10 equal-size slices. Lay *each* slice flat and cut diagonally to create 20 right-angle pieces. Place cake slices on an 11 x 9-inch baking sheet coated with non-stick vegetable oil cooking spray; set aside. In a small bowl, combine brown sugar and cinnamon, mixing well. Cut pears lengthwise into 1/4-inch slices. In a medium saucepan, combine pears, apple juice, flour, and half of the brown sugar-cinnamon mixture; bring to a boil over moderate heat. Reduce temperature and simmer until pears are tender and the liquid thickens, about 7 minutes. Cool. Reserve 2 tablespoons of liquid.

Drizzle cake slices with reserved liquid and sprinkle with remaining brown sugar-cinnamon mixture. Bake 15 minutes or until lightly browned. Remove from oven and cool.

To prepare raspberry sauce, combine raspberries, orange juice, and powdered sugar in a blender or food processor container; cover and blend or process until mixture is puréed. Spoon raspberry sauce onto dessert plates, making a "pool" in the middle of *each* plate. Arrange two cake slices, 1 inch apart, atop the sauce, with the pointed ends in the same direction. Spoon the pear mixture between the cake slices. Garnish as desired.

TIPS FOR SENSATIONAL LAYER CAKES

With a little imagination, you can dress up Sara Lee Layer Cakes for any occasion. Following, are tips to transform a plain cake into a remembered finishing touch.

QUICK AND EASY LAYER CAKE DECORATING IDEAS

Birthday Cake - *Sara Lee German Chocolate Layer Cake.* Decorate center with a circle of mini marshmallows. Fill center of circle with chocolate chips. Place white candles next to each marshmallow.

Easter Bunny Cake - *Sara Lee Coconut Layer Cake.* Mix green food coloring with grated coconut. Place colored coconut in center of cake and make a nest. Fill with colored jelly beans and position candy Easter Bunny next to nest.

Valentine Cake - *Sara Lee Double Fudge Layer Cake.* With a pastry bag and number 1 decorating tip (or with prepared decorating frosting in a writing tube), write your valentine a secret message on top of the cake.

Holiday Cake - *Sara Lee Double Fudge or Coconut Layer Cake.* Sprinkle crushed candy canes over top and sides of cake. Serve with chocolate sauce.

MAKE ANY DAY SPECIAL!
DRESS UP SARA LEE LAYER CAKES WITH:

Grated orange or lemon peel — sprinkle over cake top.

Nuts and raisins — for a sweet, nutty flavor, sprinkle on top cake slices.

Orange marmalade and fresh orange slices — spread marmalade over top of cake. Fan thinly sliced orange wedges across top of cake, press into marmalade.

Chocolate Sandwich Cookies — process cookies into crumbs and sprinkle over cake.

Caramel corn — for a child's treat, sprinkle caramel corn over cake slices.

Peanut butter cups — freeze peanut butter cup candies. While frozen, process in a blender until consistency of sand and sprinkle over cake. Frozen chocolate-covered toffee bars may be substituted.

DECORATING FROSTING

Frosting that pipes smoothly into designs is basic to successful cake decorating.

3 tablespoons butter or margarine, softened but not melted
3 tablespoons vegetable shortening, softened but not melted
3 cups powdered sugar
5 tablespoons heavy cream
1 1/2 teaspoons vanilla extract

In a medium bowl, cream butter and shortening, beating until fluffy. Beat in sugar alternately with cream and vanilla, until slightly stiff. For creative flair, add a few drops of food coloring.

Tips For Sensational Layer Cakes continued on page 58

Tips For Sensational Layer Cakes continued from page 57

TO DECORATE WITH FROSTING

Frosting tips are used with a pastry bag.

Plain tip — straight or curved lines, stems, dots, and buds. Tip sizes, for different thickness, numbered 1 through 12.

Leaf tip — leaf patterns. Tip sizes 65 through 70.

Star tip — stars and flowers. Tip sizes 13 through 22.

Rose tip — delicate flowers. Tip sizes 123 to 126.

Fluted border — number 16 tip will make an attractive border edge.

MAKE YOUR OWN PASTRY DECORATING BAG

Figure 1: Cut 12-inch squares of kitchen parchment paper or other grease-proof, strong paper (a clean grocery bag will do). Cut the squares in half from corner to corner to make triangles.

Figure 2: Hold a triangle in left hand with thumb in center of wide side of triangle; point of triangle is pointing away from you. Bring corners A and C up to corner B.

Figure 3: Firmly fold points down into the cone, opening it at the top. Snip off the bottom tip, making a hole for a decorating tip. To insert decorating tip, drop in from top of cone and wiggle through hole.

Figure 4: Spoon decorating frosting into cone, making sure to get frosting all the way into the bottom; fill cone two-thirds full with frosting. Fold over and flatten top, making corners D and E.

Figure 5: Fold corners D and E down toward center.

Figure 6: Fold top down and over. Now you're ready to decorate.

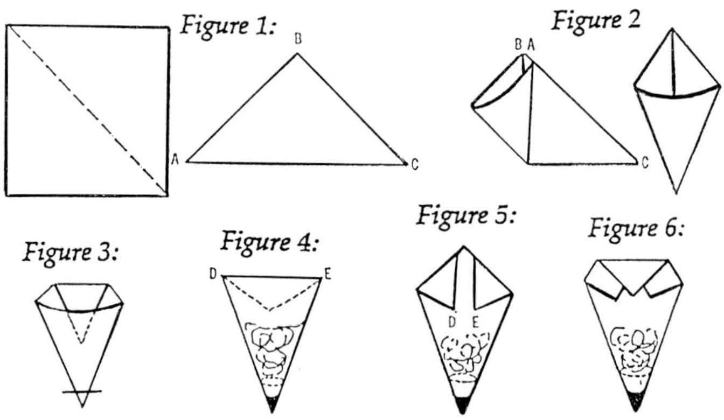

Basic Pastry Bag Decorating Technique

Always hold the pastry bag (cone) firmly at the top with one hand while the other hand gently squeezes about two-thirds the way down the bag. If your hand gets too near the tip, frosting will squeeze out the top.

4 HOLIDAY DESSERTS IN A HURRY

Holidays are always hectic.

Relief is in sight with quick, easy desserts prepared from Sara Lee baked goods that are festive, taste as scrumptious as they look, and look good enough to be given as gifts to family and friends.

Sara Lee Pound Cake is a hostess-smart dessert staple to have on hand for Holiday guests. The best Holiday news is you can make desserts as quick as a wink to create an attractive, colorful Holiday buffet for friends and family.

Even children can get in the act with easy, no-bake Holiday cookies made from Pound Cake topped with icings and sprinkles. Children will enjoy cutting out festive shapes and decorating them with their favorite topping.

Star Spangled Banner Cake

10 to 12 servings

Make your 4th of July family picnic fun and festive. Celebrate summer with this sure-to-please backyard barbeque favorite.

1 (16-ounce) family size Sara Lee Pound Cake, frozen
2 (8-ounce) packages cream cheese, softened
2 tablespoons powdered sugar
1 teaspoon vanilla extract
4 cups *fresh* strawberries, stems removed and sliced
2 cups *fresh* blueberries
2 tablespoons water (optional)

Cut Pound Cake horizontally into 4 equal-size layers. In a medium bowl, beat cream cheese until light and fluffy; add powdered sugar and vanilla, beating until smooth. Add water as necessary to achieve desired consistency.

Arrange a cake layer on a serving plate; spread with frosting. Cover with a layer of strawberries. Place a second cake layer atop the strawberries; evenly spread with frosting. Top with a layer of blueberries. Place a third cake layer atop the blueberries; repeat with frosting and strawberries. Finish with a fourth cake layer.

Frost top of cake with remaining frosting. Decorate top to resemble an American flag. Place blueberries in the upper left corner. Make flag stripes with alternating horizontal rows of strawberry slices and frosting.

Selma Knief
Chicago, Illinois

FREDA'S EASY POUND CAKE STRUDEL

6 servings

Centuries ago in Hungary, the flaky nut and fruit-filled roll of paper-thin pastry called strudel was invented. The strudel is perfection served warm from the oven with a dusting of powdered sugar.

Preheat oven to 350°F.

1 (16-ounce) family size Sara Lee Pound Cake, thawed
1 (12-ounce) jar apricot preserves
1/2 cup chopped pecans
1/2 cup dark seedless raisins
1 teaspoon cinnamon
1/2 cup butter or margarine, melted
1 (16-ounce) package phyllo dough, frozen

Crumble Pound Cake into a food processor or blender container; cover and process or blend until fine crumbs are formed. Transfer to a large bowl. Add apricot preserves, pecans, raisins, and cinnamon, mixing well; set aside. (This filling is enough for three strudels. Separate filling into three equal parts. Refrigerate excess, covered, for later use.)

Remove phyllo dough from freezer and unwrap. Place frozen phyllo in a microwave oven between two cloth (or paper) towels; microwave at defrost power for 2 minutes. Turn over phyllo and microwave again for 2 minutes. Remove and gently unroll. If dough doesn't unroll, continue microwaving at defrost power for 30 second intervals, until dough opens completely. For each strudel, gently separate 4 to 6 sheets, removing them from the remaining phyllo dough, being careful not to tear them.

Lay sheets of dough onto a large clean work surface sprinkled lightly with flour. With a pastry brush, gently brush butter onto *each* sheet to keep moist. Stack the buttered phyllo sheets; sprinkle one-third reserved strudel filling over a 1/2-inch wide strip at one end of the stacked phyllo sheets. Starting at the filling end of dough, gently roll dough jelly roll-style, sprinkle again with filling, and roll again. Sprinkle filling a third and final time and roll to the end of the dough. Gently lift strudel, seam-side down, onto a greased baking sheet. Brush with remaining butter and bake 15 to 20 minutes or until golden brown. Cool and slice. Strudel may be reheated or toasted, if desired.

Freda Shulruff
Wilmette, Illinois

DIPLOMAT PUDDING

16 servings

This pudding makes a delectable Holiday dessert centerpiece. Slice and serve at the table with extra chocolate glaze drizzled over each piece.

4 (10 3/4-ounce) Sara Lee Pound Cakes, frozen
5 tablespoons crème de cacao liqueur or chocolate sauce
2 1/4 cups milk
1/2 cup short-grain rice
1/2 cup sugar
1/2 cup cocoa powder
1 cup heavy cream
2 tablespoons powdered sugar
1/4 teaspoon vanilla extract

Chocolate Glaze

10 ounces semi-sweet chocolate
1/2 cup heavy cream
2 tablespoons unsalted butter or margarine
2 tablespoons sugar
Candied or *fresh* seedless orange slices for garnish

Cut *each* Pound Cake horizontally into 6 thin equal-size layers, making 24 layers. Coat the inside of a 12-cup bundt pan with non-stick vegetable oil cooking spray. Place 4 cake layers around the bottom of the mold. Use the fifth layer for pieces to fill any cracks. Press cake firmly into bottom of the mold. Sprinkle cake in pan and remaining cake layers with crème de cacao; cover and set aside.

To prepare pudding, combine milk, rice, and sugar in a medium saucepan; bring to a boil, stirring frequently, over moderate heat. Reduce heat, continue cooking, stirring often, until liquid is absorbed and rice is tender, about 20 minutes. Remove from heat; blend in cocoa. Cool. Spread a layer of rice mixture over cake in mold. Top rice mixture with another layer of cake.

In a chilled, deep, medium bowl, beat cream with chilled beaters until stiff peaks form. Spread whipped cream, 1/2-inch thick, over cake layer; repeat another cake layer and cover with remaining rice mixture. Finish with another cake layer. Cover and chill in refrigerator at least 6 hours before serving.

To prepare chocolate glaze, combine chocolate, cream, butter, and sugar in a medium saucepan; stir over moderate heat until blended and smooth. Transfer glaze to a bowl; cool in refrigerator. Run a knife around the inside edge of the mold to loosen cake. Unmold cake onto a serving platter. Pour chocolate glaze over top of cake, allowing glaze to drizzle down the sides; allow to stand until chocolate glaze firms-up. To serve, cut slices, place on dessert plates, and garnish with candied or *fresh* orange slices.

CROWNING GLORY FRUITCAKE

12 servings

The following fruit cakes are updated 90's versions that are light in taste and texture. They can be used together as the centerpiece of a Holiday buffet, or given individually as gifts.

2 (10 3/4-ounce) Sara Lee Pound Cakes, frozen
1 (29-ounce) can sliced peaches, drained (reserve juice)
1/4 cup apple jelly
1 tablespoon hot water
Assorted candied fruits for garnish

Cut both Pound Cakes vertically into *very* thin slices. (If they fall apart, it's okay.)

Press cake slices firmly into a 10-inch bundt pan or crown mold, one layer at a time. Line pan or mold with slices over the bottom and up the sides, forming one layer. Lightly brush cake slices with peach juice. Repeat layering process four more times. Starting with the fifth layer, start pushing peach slices into the layers. Continue the process until the pan or mold is full. Cover and refrigerate for 8 hours.

To unmold, dip bottom of pan or mold into warm water for 30 seconds. Run a knife around the inside edge of mold to loosen cake; invert onto a serving plate. Shake gently to release cake.

In a 1-cup measure, combine apple jelly and hot water, blending well; set aside. Decorate the cake with candied fruits and lightly brush entire cake with the apple jelly mixture to achieve a shiny glaze.

RING IN THE NEW YEAR FRUITCAKE

12 servings

3 (10 3/4-ounce) Sara Lee Pound Cakes, frozen
3 (3.4-ounce) packages vanilla-flavored instant pudding and pie filling mix
3 1/3 cups cold milk
2 tablespoons Grand Marnier liqueur or orange juice
3 cups chopped assorted candied fruit

Cut Pound Cakes into small chunks. Place cake chunks in a blender or food processor container; cover and blend or process until coarse crumbs are formed. Transfer to a large bowl; set aside.

Fruitcake recipes continued on page 68

Fruitcake recipes continued from page 66

In a medium bowl, combine pudding mix, milk, and Grand Marnier; beat at high speed of an electric mixer until mixture is slightly stiff. Fold pudding and 2 cups candied fruit into cake crumbs. Gently spoon mixture into a 12-cup bundt pan or mold sprayed with non-stick vegetable oil cooking spray; cover with plastic wrap and freeze at least 4 hours.

Invert fruitcake onto a serving platter; shake mold slightly to remove cake. (If the cake doesn't come out easily, dip the bottom of the mold in warm water.) Decorate the cake with remaining candied fruit. Serve immediately.

NUTCRACKER SWEET FRUITCAKE

(Rectangular Cake)
10 servings

Send Holiday cheer to family and friends. When covered tightly in plastic wrap and boxed, this cake can be mailed.

1 (10 3/4-ounce) Sara Lee Pound Cake, frozen
1 (12-ounce) jar apricot jam
3/4 cup walnuts, coarsely chopped
Assorted candied fruits for garnish
1/4 cup apple jelly
1 tablespoon hot water

Cut Pound Cake horizontally in half. Spread apricot jam over bottom cake layer and sprinkle with crushed walnuts. Place second layer over walnuts; thinly spread remaining apricot jam over top and sides of cake. Decorate with candied fruits.

In a 1-cup measure, combine apple jelly and hot water, blending well. Lightly brush apple glaze over cake and fruit. (The apple glaze makes the cake shine and helps to set the candied fruits.) Cake need not be refrigerated.

No-Bake Holiday Cookies

about 12 cookies

Now, thanks to Sara Lee Pound Cake, decorated cookies, so good even Santa will like them and so quick and easy they accommodate the most hectic schedule, are possible. It's as simple as slice, spread, and sprinkle. They're so easy children can make them and, when personalized with candy letters, they can be used for place cards on your Holiday table.

1 (10 3/4-ounce) Sara Lee Pound Cake, frozen
1 (8-ounce) container prepared chocolate frosting or other favorite-flavor frosting
Sprinkles, cake decorations, prepared tube decorator icings, and/or hard candies

Cut Pound Cake horizontally into 3 or 4 equal-size layers, depending on desired thickness. Use a variety of cookie cutters to make shapes; decorate with prepared frostings, sprinkles, candy letters, and shapes.

Holiday Surprise Balls

about 32 cookies

These traditional Holiday cookies make a welcome hostess gift and are a compliment to any Holiday buffet.

1 (10 3/4-ounce) Sara Lee Pound Cake, thawed
1 (3 1/2-ounce) package pecan pieces
1/2 cup candied red cherries, chopped
1/3 cup Amaretto liqueur
1/4 cup powdered sugar
1/2 teaspoon vanilla extract
Additional powdered sugar, as needed

Cut Pound Cake into pieces and place in a food processor or blender container; cover and process or blend into fine crumbs. In a medium bowl, combine crumbled cake and the next 5 ingredients, mixing well. Cover and chill mixture thoroughly in the refrigerator.

Shape mixture into 1/2 to 3/4-inch diameter balls. On a sheet of wax paper, roll balls in additional powdered sugar, coating *each* well. Store cookies in an airtight container.

Charlene Wolthausen
Carrollton, Texas

5 EASY SWEET TREATS

Snacking is an American tradition. Simply put, we love in-between-meal treats. When you want to satisfy that craving for a sweet that's in your hand one second and in your mouth the next, here are simple, delectable treats you can prepare in advance.

Keep your copy of AMERICA'S FAVORITE DESSERTS on hand in the kitchen so you can treat everyone to a delightfully different snack. Then, something wonderful is always around whenever your sweet tooth strikes.

Easy Triple Layer Bars

24 bars

Preheat oven to 350°F.
Grease and flour a 13 x 9 x 2-inch baking pan

1 (10 3/4-ounce) Sara Lee Pound Cake, thawed
2 1/2 cups quick-cooking rolled oats
1 (12-ounce) package semi-sweet chocolate chips
1 (14-ounce) can sweetened condensed milk

Cut Pound Cake horizontally into 5 equal-size layers. Arrange cake layers, completely covering bottom of pan. Sprinkle rolled oats evenly over cake. Sprinkle chocolate chips evenly over oats. Pour sweetened condensed milk over chocolate chips. Bake 25 minutes. Remove from oven and immediately "rake" top lightly with the tines of a fork to blend toppings. Cool 30 minutes. Cut into 24 bars. Serve warm or at room temperature.

Karen Gerhart
Bloomfield Hills, Michigan

Harriet's Pyramids

16 pieces

Just right for after-school snacks with a glass of milk.

1 (10 3/4-ounce) Sara Lee Pound Cake, frozen
1 (10-ounce) jar white dipping chocolate
1 (10-ounce) jar milk, or semi-sweet, or bittersweet dipping chocolate
1/2 cup chopped pecans or blanched almonds
3/4 cup chocolate sprinkles

Remove the browned top from Pound Cake and discard *(or eat!)*. Cut cake vertically into 8 equal-size slices; lay slices flat and cut *each* in half diagonally to make 16 angle pieces.

If dipping chocolate is packaged in microwave-safe jars, remove lids, and melt in the microwave oven according to package directions. Remove from microwave and immediately begin dipping cake pieces, pointed ends extended halfway into the various chocolates. Allow chocolate to harden slightly before dipping into another chocolate, nuts, or sprinkles. Place dipped cake pieces on wax paper; allow to cool until firm.

Harriet Hanson
Chicago, Illinois

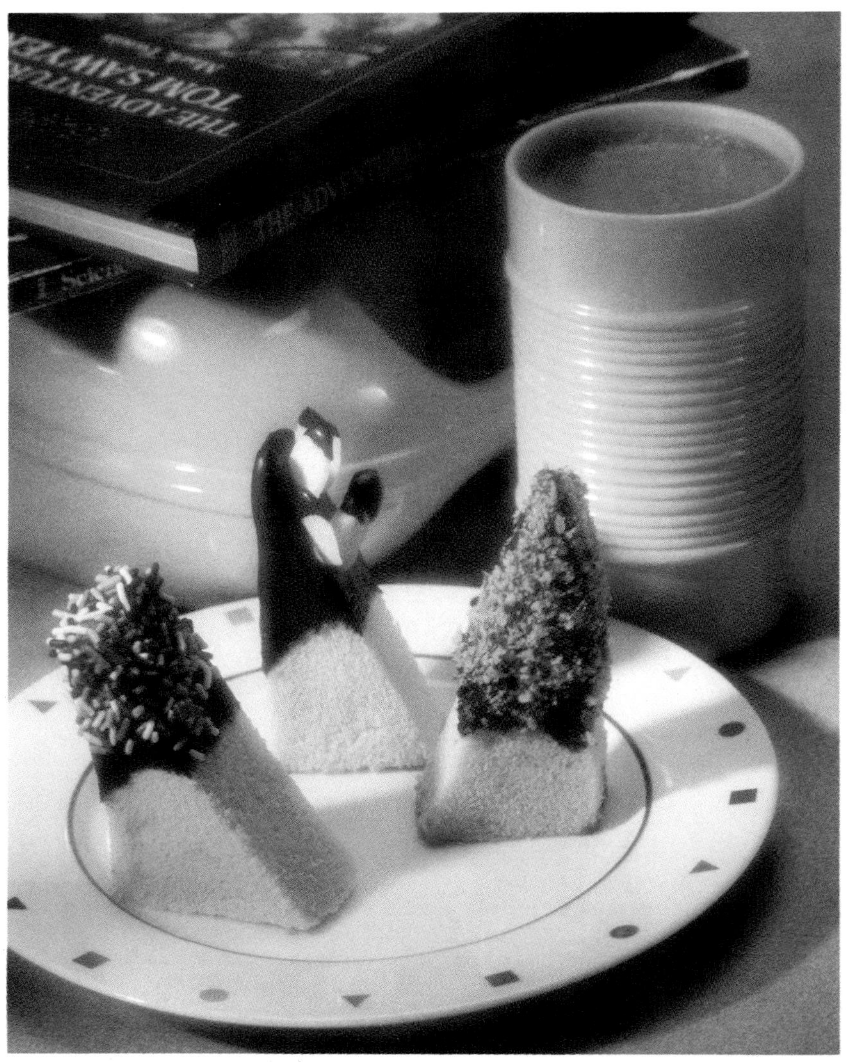

Peanut Butter Dots

18 to 20 cookies

For crisp texture, bake for an additional 5 to 7 minutes.

Preheat oven to 350°F.

1 (10 3/4-ounce) Sara Lee Pound Cake, thawed
1 egg
1 cup crunchy-style peanut butter
1/4 cup semi-sweet chocolate chips

Crumble Pound Cake into a food processor or blender container; cover and process or blend until fine crumbs are formed. Transfer to a medium bowl; add egg and peanut butter, mixing well. Butter and flour hands or wear smooth plastic gloves; pinch off small pieces of dough and roll between the palms to make 1/2-inch diameter balls. Arrange balls on a greased baking sheet; flatten with the tines of a fork. Bake 15 minutes or until lightly browned. Immediately upon removing from oven, gently push a chocolate chip into the center of *each* cookie.

Apricot Squares

8 squares

Preheat oven to 350°F.
Grease and flour an 8 x 8 x 2-inch baking pan

1 (10 3/4-ounce) Sara Lee Pound Cake, thawed
1 egg
2 tablespoons butter or margarine, melted
1 (12-ounce) jar apricot preserves
10 to 15 dried apricots, finely chopped
1/4 cup chopped walnuts or pecans

Crumble Pound Cake into a food processor or blender container; cover and process or blend until fine crumbs are formed. Add egg and butter, mixing well. Evenly press dough into baking pan. Spread preserves evenly over dough and sprinkle with chopped apricots and nuts. Bake 40 minutes. Remove from oven and cool before cutting into squares.

TOFFEE SQUARES

20 squares

Have plenty of these on hand to satisfy your sweet tooth.

Preheat oven to 350°F.

1 (10 3/4-ounce) Sara Lee Pound Cake, frozen
1/2 cup butter or margarine
1 cup light brown sugar, firmly packed
1 cup semi-sweet chocolate chips
1/2 cup chopped pecans or walnuts

Cut Pound Cake vertically into 10 equal-size slices. Arrange cake slices on a broiler rack; broil, 8 to 10 inches from heat source, until lightly browned on *each* side. Or, toast cake slices in a toaster oven until lightly browned.

Combine butter and brown sugar in a small saucepan; stir over moderate heat for 3 minutes. Arrange cake slices on an ungreased baking sheet. Spoon half the brown sugar mixture over cake slices, dividing evenly. Bake 5 minutes. Remove from oven and sprinkle chocolate chips, nuts, and remaining brown sugar mixture over cake slices; return to oven and bake 10 to 15 minutes until chocolate melts. Remove from oven and spread melted chocolate evenly over slices. Cut *each* slice in half and allow to cool.

MOCHA-CHOCOLATE CHEESE SQUARES

16 pieces

For a cool bite, serve partially frozen. (Place in container and freeze. Remove from freezer and let stand for 20 minutes before serving).

1 (17-ounce) Sara Lee Original Cream Cheesecake, frozen
1 (10 3/4-ounce) Sara Lee Pound Cake, frozen

Mocha Chocolate Glaze

8 ounces semi-sweet chocolate
1/3 cup heavy cream
1 tablespoon butter or margarine
1/4 cup strong-brewed coffee
2 teaspoons powdered sugar

With a sharp knife, remove the crust from the bottom of the Original Cream Cheesecake and discard. Cut Cheesecake in half horizontally. Stack the halves, one atop the other; slice vertically into thirds. Repeat in opposite direction, making 18 total pieces. Set aside.

Cut Pound Cake horizontally into 4 equal-size layers. Stack the 4 layers atop *each* other. Vertically slice cake into fourths. Cut the 4-layered cake sections in half to make 32 Pound Cake squares.

In a medium saucepan, combine chocolate, cream, and butter; stir over moderate heat, melting chocolate and butter. Stir in coffee and powdered sugar. Refrigerate for 5 minutes to cool.

Place a Cheesecake square between 2 Pound Cake squares, sandwich-style; set on a wire rack or wax paper. Repeat until 16 sandwich squares have been assembled. *(Two Cheesecake squares will be left over - why not pop them into your mouth!)* Drizzle Mocha Chocolate Glaze over *each* square, allowing chocolate mixture to drizzle down all sides. Refrigerate 30 minutes before serving.

6 CHEF'S CHOICE

To pick the five finalist recipes competing for the coveted title of America's Favorite Dessert, Sara Lee Bakery convened seven of the top chefs in the U.S.A. for a lively afternoon of tasting at New York's prestigious Mark Hotel.

America's best chefs selected the five recipes from a group of exciting, creative, and delicious contest entries.

On hand to pick the final candidates were: Chef Joachim Splichal, owner of Patina Restaurant in Los Angeles; Jean-Louis Palladin, chef of Jean-Louis at the Watergate in Washington, D.C.; Philippe Boulot, executive chef of New York's Mark Hotel; Chef Mary Beth Liccioni, co-owner of Le Francais in Chicago; Jacques Torres, pastry chef of Le Cirque in New York; Nancy Silverton, pastry chef and co-owner of Campanile in Los Angeles; and Christopher Gross, chef and owner of Christopher's in Phoenix.

These luminaries of the culinary world have a few ideas of their own to share. Here are some of their secrets for making Sara Lee baked goods a special dessert experience.

PUDDING WITH ALMONDS

8 servings

Preheat oven to 350°F.

1 (10 3/4-ounce) Sara Lee Pound Cake, frozen

Crème Anglaise

2 quarts (8 cups) milk
1 teaspoon vanilla extract
6 egg yolks
3/4 cup sugar

1 cup slivered blanched almonds

Cut Pound Cake vertically into 3/4-inch slices, set aside. In a large saucepan, bring milk to a boil; reduce heat and simmer 1 minute. In a medium bowl, whisk egg yolks and sugar together until creamy. Gradually add egg yolk mixture to milk, stirring constantly. Continue to heat until foam begins to form; remove from heat and let cool.

Arrange Pound Cake slices in bottom of a 9-inch round spring-form pan. Spread almonds over cake slices. Pour half of Crème Anglaise over cake. Bake for 15 to 20 minutes. Refrigerate for 2 hours or until cool. When ready to serve, garnish with remainder of Crème Anglaise.

Variation: Add color with fruit coulis. To make fruit coulis, combine 1 cup strawberries, raspberries, or blueberries in blender or food processor container with 3 tablespoons water and 2 tablespoons sugar; cover and blend or process until puréed. Press sauce through strainer to remove seeds. Spread coulis over or around individual servings of pudding.

Jean-Louis Palladin, Jean-Louis At The Watergate
Washington, D.C.

Pictured from left to right: *Jacques Torres, Le Cirque; Philippe Boulot, The Mark Hotel; Nancy Silverton, Campanile; Jean-Louis Palladin, Jean-Louis at the Watergate; Joachim Splichal, Patina; Christopher Gross, Christopher's; Mary Beth Liccioni, Le Francais*

Nancy Silverton
La Brea Bakery
ACHIM

BREAD PUDDING

6 servings

Preheat oven to 325°F.
Butter a 2-quart baking dish

2 cups heavy cream
2 cups milk
2 teaspoons vanilla extract
8 eggs
1 1/3 cups sugar
1 (10 3/4-ounce) Sara Lee Pound Cake, thawed
1/4 cup golden seedless raisins
1/2 cup apricot preserves, warmed

Combine cream, milk, and vanilla in a medium saucepan; scald over moderate heat. Remove and set aside. In a large bowl, beat together eggs and sugar. Gradually stir cream mixture into egg mixture, stirring constantly.

Cut Pound Cake vertically into 10 equal-size slices. Sprinkle raisins over bottom of baking dish. Layer cake slices, shingle-style (over lapping), into bottom of dish. Pour warm cream-egg mixture over cake. Place baking dish in a *bain marie* (pan of hot water); add enough water to fill *bain marie* halfway up side of baking dish. Bake 30 to 40 minutes. Remove from oven and let cool.

To warm preserves, heat, loosely covered, in a microwave oven for 25 seconds at high power. Or, warm in the top of a double boiler over simmering water until preserves begin to thin. Brush top of pudding with warm preserves and serve.

Philippe and Susan Boulot, The Mark Hotel
New York, New York

TARTE TARTÌN

8 servings

Preheat oven to 400° F.
Coat a 15x10x1-inch baking pan with non-stick vegetable oil cooking spray

1 (10 3/4-ounce) Sara Lee Pound Cake, frozen
1 cup sugar
1/4 cup water
8 medium cooking apples , peeled, cored and *each* cut in half
1 pint (2 cups) vanilla ice cream

Cut Pound Cake vertically into 8 equal-size slices. In a medium saucepan, combine sugar and water. Cook, stirring frequently, until sugar is caramelized. Let cool. Arrange apple halves in baking pan; pour half of the caramel sauce over fruit. Cover pan and bake for 45 minutes. Remove from oven and let cool. Arrange a slice of Pound Cake on *each* plate; place two warm apple halves on *each* cake slice. Top with a scoop of ice cream and serve with remaining caramel sauce.

Jacques Torres, Le Cirque
New York, New York

CRISPY FRUIT DELIGHT

4 servings

1 (10 3/4-ounce) Sara Lee Pound Cake, frozen
1 (3.4-ounce) package vanilla pudding and pie filling mix (not instant) prepared to package directions
2 cups sliced *fresh* fruit
1 cup heavy cream
1 tablespoon sugar
1 tablespoon *fresh* lemon juice

Cut Pound Cake vertically into 12 slices. Toast on both sides. Prepare vanilla pudding and allow to cool. In chilled medium bowl, beat the cream with chilled beaters until stiff peaks form; cover and refrigerate. In a blender or food processor, purée 1 cup of fruit with sugar and lemon juice; set aside.

Fold whipped cream into pudding. On each of four dessert plates, place a slice of Pound Cake; spread with pudding mixture. Top with fruit. Repeat next two layers, ending with fruit. Spoon reserved fruit around dessert.

Mary Beth Liccioni, Le Francais
Chicago, Illinois

Vanilla Bean Ice Cream

10 servings

3 vanilla beans, *each* cut in half
2 cups milk
2 cups heavy cream
2 cups sugar
10 egg yolks
1/2 cup *fresh* strawberries, stemmed and mashed with a fork
1/2 (10 3/4-ounce) Sara Lee Pound Cake, thawed, cut into cubes

In a medium saucepan, combine vanilla beans, milk, cream, and 1 cup sugar; bring to a boil. Remove from heat. In a medium bowl, beat together eggs and remaining sugar. Gradually stir egg mixture into milk mixture, stirring constantly. Return to heat and cook until mixture thickens. Remove from heat. Remove vanilla beans; slice open and scrape seeds into cream mixture; discard pods.

Process in ice cream machine according to manufacturer's directions until creamy, about 10 to 15 minutes, depending upon machine. When ice cream is almost finished, add strawberries and Pound Cake to ice cream. Process until ice cream is ready. Remove from ice cream maker and serve immediately or store, tightly covered, in freezer.

Joachim Splichal, Patina
Los Angeles, California

Millefeuille Of Pound Cake With Fresh Passion Fruits

8 servings

1 (10 3/4-ounce) Sara Lee Pound Cake, frozen
1/2 cup sugar
3 cups heavy cream
2 1/4 cups passion fruit juice
2 cups *fresh* fruit, stemmed and thinly sliced kiwi or blueberries
Fresh mint leaves for garnish

Cut Pound Cake horizontally into 5 to 6 layers. Place slices onto a baking sheet sprayed with non-stick vegetable oil spray. Sprinkle slices with sugar and caramelize under broiler, broiling 6 to 8 inches from heat source. Remove from oven and cool.

In a medium bowl beat cream until soft peaks form. Add 1/4 cup passion fruit juice and continue beating until stiff peaks form.

To assemble, place 1 layer of Pound Cake on a serving platter; top with cream and fruit. Repeat layers until complete, ending with a layer of plain toasted Pound Cake.

To serve, present Millefeuille and slice gently at the table, into 8 vertical slices. Place on individual dessert plates. Surround *each* slice with 1/4 cup passion fruit juice.

Christopher Gross, Christopher's
Phoenix, Arizona

SAUTÉED STRAWBERRIES

8 servings

1 1/2 cups sugar
1/2 cup water
4 black peppercorns
2 cloves
1 cinnamon stick
1/2 teaspoon nutmeg
1 (750-liter) bottle Beaujolais wine
1 (10 3/4-ounce) Sara Lee Pound Cake, frozen
2 pints *fresh* strawberries, stemmed and sliced
Whipped cream for garnish

Combine the first 6 ingredients in a medium saucepan; bring to a boil. Add wine and continue to boil, reducing volume by one-third. Remove from heat.

Transfer half of red wine syrup to a large sauté pan and bring to a boil. Add half of the strawberries; sauté until syrup thickens and strawberries are transparent. Remove from heat and repeat process with remaining syrup and strawberries.

Cut Pound Cake vertically into 16 slices. Place slices on a baking sheet and toast under broiler, 6 to 8 inches from heat source, turning, until golden brown on both sides. Arrange two slices per person on individual dessert plates and artfully pour sautéed strawberries over *each* serving. Garnish with whipped cream and serve immediately.

Nancy Silverton, Campanile
Los Angeles, California

Apple Cinnamon Raisin Cake

10 Servings

Preheat oven to 300°F.
Spray an 8-inch round layer cake pan with non-stick vegetable oil cooking spray

1 (10 3/4-ounce) Sara Lee Pound Cake, frozen
2 tart cooking apples, peeled and cored
1 cup apple juice
1/4 cup dark seedless raisins
2 tablespoons sugar
2 tablespoons flour
2 tablespoons cinnamon
Fresh seedless orange slices for garnish

Cut Pound Cake vertically into 10 equal-size slices. Lay *each* slice flat and cut again diagonally, creating 20 right-angle pieces; set aside.

Cut the apples into small cubes. In a medium saucepan, combine the apples, apple juice, raisins, 1 tablespoon sugar, and flour, mixing well. Bring mixture to a boil, reduce heat and continue to cook apples until they are tender and the liquid is thick, about 10 minutes. Remove from heat and allow to cool.

In a 1-cup measure, combine the remaining 1 tablespoon sugar and cinnamon, mixing well. Sprinkle 1 tablespoon of the cinnamon mixture over the bottom of the pan; reserve remaining mixture.

In the bottom of the pan, form a circle of cake pieces by arranging 10 pieces with the pointed ends towards the center. Lightly press the pieces together. Spoon the apple mixture over cake slices, reserving some of the liquid.

With the remaining cake slices, form another circle over the apple-raisin mixture, like a sandwich; lightly press pieces together. Spoon the reserved liquid over cake and sprinkle with remaining cinnamon-sugar mixture. Bake 1 hour. Remove from oven and allow to cool in pan. Garnish *each* serving with an orange slice.

Chef Robert Del Grande, Cafe Annie
Houston, Texas

7 BRUNCH GETS EVEN BETTER

When the weekend finally arrives and your morning stretches into a relaxed midday meal, brunch can be a wonderful taste experience with friends and family.

Following are inventive brunch recipes that will sweeten your day without a lot of fuss.

Porcupine Brunch Cake

8 servings

This quick and easy treat is perfect for cozy Sunday mornings with the newspaper and a good cup of coffee. To fill the air with the luscious aroma of cinnamon, pop the finished cake under a broiler (8 to 10 inches from heat source) until the almonds are lightly browned, about 3 minutes.

1 (10 3/4-ounce) Sara Lee Pound Cake, frozen
1 (10-ounce) jar apricot jam
1 1/2 cups granola
1 cup slivered blanched almonds
Cinnamon as desired for garnish

Cut the Pound Cake horizontally into 3 equal-size layers. Place 1 cake layer on an oven-proof serving plate. Spread with one-third of the jam and sprinkle with one-third of the granola.

Repeat process for a second layer. Top with a third cake layer. Evenly spread top of third layer with remaining jam.

Arrange almonds, standing on end, close together over the top of the cake, to resemble porcupine's quills. Sprinkle entire cake with cinnamon.

Christopher Manenti
Saddle River, New Jersey

Cosmo time

French Toast Bananas Foster

4 main-dish or 8 side-dish servings

Reminiscent of New Orleans, this also makes an impressive dessert when flambéed with brandy.

1 (10 3/4-ounce) Sara Lee Pound Cake, frozen
3/4 cup light brown sugar, firmly packed
1/4 cup heavy cream
1/4 cup butter or margarine
1 tablespoon coconut-flavored rum or 1/2 teaspoon coconut extract
1 teaspoon vanilla extract
1/4 cup pecan halves
3 large bananas
3 eggs, beaten
Cinnamon and powdered sugar for garnish

Cut Pound Cake into 8 vertical slices; set aside. In a 2-quart saucepan, combine brown sugar, cream, butter, rum, and vanilla. Cook, stirring constantly, over moderate heat until sugar is melted and sauce is smooth. Peel and slice bananas diagonally; gently fold into sauce. Fold in pecans. Keep sauce warm over low heat.

Dip Pound Cake slices into beaten eggs; pan-fry egg-dipped cake slices in a large skillet, sprayed with non-stick vegetable oil cooking spray, over moderate heat, about 1 to 2 minutes per side, or until crispy and lightly browned. Allow 2 slices per person as a main-dish or 1 slice as a side dish. Arrange slices on plates; spoon sauce over *each* and sprinkle with cinnamon and powdered sugar.

Esta E. Lynch
Columbus, Ohio

HEARTS IN A FRAME

2 servings

Make romantic plans for weekend mornings with a quick romantic brunch that's heart-felt.

1 (10 3/4-ounce) Sara Lee Pound Cake, frozen
4 egg whites, at room temperature
1 tablespoon minced fresh or 2 teaspoons dried chives
Pinch of paprika
1 seedless medium orange, peeled and thinly sliced, for garnish

Cut Pound Cake horizontally in half; return one half to freezer. Cut remaining half vertically into 2 equal-size slices. Using a heart-shaped cookie cutter, approximately 1 1/2-inches in diameter, cut out a heart in the middle of *each* cake slice; set aside.

In a deep, medium bowl, beat egg whites and spices together until frothy. Place cake slices and heart-shaped cut-outs in a heated skillet coated with non-stick vegetable oil cooking spray. Fill the hole in the cake slices with egg white mixture; cover and cook over low heat until egg white in *each* is firm. Turn over cake slices and heart shapes; continue to brown lightly, about 1 minute. Garnish *each* serving with orange slices and serve with a favorite Champagne or herbal tea.

CHEESECAKE CRÊPES

6 servings

*For a scrumptious dessert variation,
serve with a scoop of sorbet or ice cream.*

2 (17-ounce) Sara Lee Original Cream Cheesecakes, thawed
12 prepared crêpes (see note)
1 cup fresh or frozen sliced strawberries
1 cup fresh or frozen blueberries
2 cups heavy cream
4 teaspoons powdered sugar
1/2 teaspoon vanilla extract
Additional powdered sugar for garnish

Cut Cheesecakes into small pieces and place in a blender or food processor container; cover and blend or process until smooth. Transfer to a medium bowl. Fold in 1/2 cup strawberries and 1/2 cup blueberries; set aside.

In a chilled, deep, medium bowl, combine cream, powdered sugar, and vanilla; beat with chilled beaters at high speed of an electric mixer until stiff peaks form. Fold whipped cream into Cheesecake mixture.

Heat individual crêpes according to package directions. While still warm, place 2 crêpes per person on individual serving plates. Spoon Cheesecake-whipped cream mixture across the center of *each* crêpe; roll crêpes jelly roll-style, placing seam-side down on the plates. Garnish with remaining berries and sprinkle with powdered sugar.

Note: Prepared crêpes can be found in the refrigerated or frozen sections of most supermarkets.

GRANDMA SHEPPIE'S BANANA CAKE

6 to 8 servings

For an attractive brunch presentation, slice and serve on a platter decorated with fresh orange wedges. Also a welcome surprise in a lunch box.

Preheat oven to 350°F.
Grease and flour an 8 x 3 3/4 x 2 1/2-inch loaf pan

1 (16-ounce) family size Sara Lee Pound Cake, thawed
3/4 cup mashed ripe bananas
1 teaspoon baking soda
1/2 cup semi-sweet chocolate chips (see note)
1/2 cup chopped pecans or walnuts
2 egg whites, at room temperature
1/4 teaspoon cream of tartar

Crumble Pound Cake into a food processor or blender container; cover and process or blend until fine crumbs are formed. Transfer to a medium bowl. Add bananas and baking soda, mixing well. Stir in chocolate chips and nuts.

In a small bowl, combine egg whites and cream of tartar; beat until stiff peaks form. Carefully fold egg whites into cake mixture. Spoon into pan, spreading evenly. Bake 60 minutes. Allow to cool before removing cake from pan. Individual slices may be toasted, if desired.

Note: 1/2 cup dark seedless raisins may be substituted for chocolate chips.

Rosalyn "Sheppie" Baer
Ft. Lauderdale, Florida

INDEX

Nobody doesn't like Sara Lee, so why not share this collection of dessert recipes with friends and family. It makes a delicious, thoughtful and affordable gift.

To order additional copies of AMERICA'S FAVORITE DESSERTS, while supplies last, just call toll-free 1-800-766-8009 from 9 a.m. to 5 p.m. Eastern Standard Time, Monday through Friday. Or write to:

AMERICA'S FAVORITE DESSERTS
P.O. Box 1248
Chesapeake, VA 23327

$5.95 plus $2 for postage and handling.
Or $4.95 plus $2 postage and handling when accompanied by two UPC code symbols from any Sara Lee Bakery product.

Visa and MasterCard accepted.

Make checks payable (do not send cash) to AMERICA'S FAVORITE DESSERTS.

Allow 3 weeks for delivery